HOW TO WRITE
A NOVEL
IN 10 EASY STEPS

AUTORISSIMO

Quick and easy guide
for writing and planning a novel

Eva Alton

Original title: *Cómo escribir un libro paso a paso*
Copyright © 2023 Eva Alton
Copyright © 2024 of the English translation: Eva Alton

This book is dedicated to Riccardo.

All rights reserved.
First English edition.

Edited by: Sheila Grimes

www.writersunlock.com
www.autorissimo.com

HOW TO WRITE
A NOVEL
IN 10 EASY STEPS

Table of Contents:

BEFORE WE START...5

What can this book do for you? 5

Is this book *only* for writing novels?.........................6

The structure of a novel, the reader's experience, and excuses from those who don't want to study.......................8

Write your novel using the *Autorissimo* method...............14

What is this method about?..15

Who am I to tell you all of this?................................16

Chapter One..21

The Importance of Planning..................................21

Why plan a novel before writing it?.............................21

But... do I really have to plan everything before starting? 24

Pantsers, Plotters, and How *Not* to End Up Like Hansel and Gretel...25

Today's task: step 1 30

Chapter Two...31

Find your genre...31

What are literary genres, and how can they be useful?.. 32

The most popular literary genres 34

Today's task: step 2 39

Chapter Three **41**

The secret sauce **41**

WHAT HAPPENS IN THE STORY?...44

Today's task: step 3 ....**51**

Chapter Four **53**

When Characters Come to Life **53**

THE *WHO* OF YOUR STORY...53

The character arc and *Character Metamorphosis*..............55

Character metamorphosis for series.....................................60

Physical appearance..63

Your protagonist's personality...65

Character Profile..66

Today's task: Step 4..**76**

Chapter Five **83**

The ideal breeding ground **83**

The Perfect Setting for Your Story 83

Location Sheet..90

Today's Tasks: Step 5..**96**

Chapter Six...**101**

The Pillars of Your Novel **101**

The *WhoWhereCon* Worksheet................................103

Today's task: Step 6 ...... **109**

Chapter Seven **111**
Writing a great synopsis **111**

Tricks for Writing an Intriguing Synopsis 114
6 Essential Characteristics of a Good Synopsis 115

Task for today: Step 7 ...... **119**

Chapter Eight **121**

Common Narrative Structures 124
The *Chrysalis* Plot 128
Narrative Metamorphosis Segments 130
Explanation of each segment and its key points 135
Examples of the CHRYSALIS plot in use 142
"Snow White" 142
"Little Women" by Louisa May Alcott 143
"The Da Vinci Code" by Dan Brown 144

Today's Task: Step 8 ...... **146**

Chapter Nine **148**
Chapters and Scenes **148**

Developing the Chrysalis Structure into Chapters and Scenes: 148
How Many Pages Do I Have to Write? 148
Let's Talk Numbers 149
How Many Chapters and How Long? 151

How to Divide the Story into Chapters................................152

The Importance of the First Chapter................................153

How to Divide Chapters into Scenes:................................155

Today's Task: Step 9................................**160**

Chapter Ten................................**162**

Underlying themes................................**162**

The heart of storytelling................................162

Examples of underlying themes................................165

5 Steps to include an underlying message in your story

................................165

Today's Task: Step 10................................**169**

Conclusion................................**170**

Key Concepts................................170

And... what now?................................174

FIND ME HERE:................................**175**

Are you looking for more books like this?................................175

OTHER TITLES BY EVA ALTON................................**176**

Bibliography................................**177**

Works mentioned in this manual:................................177

Extra Chapter................................**180**

I've got something for you...................................**180**

BEFORE WE START...

What can this book do for you?

"

The purpose of this manual is to assist you in turning your dream of writing a novel from start to finish into a reality.

A couple of years ago, I moved to a new house. The house was completely empty, so much so that there weren't even faucets or sinks in it. I dreamed of creating a home within those walls, but my budget was... *limited*, to put it mildly. Just like most people of my generation, I ordered a bunch of flat-pack furniture, the kind that requires assembling, with hundreds of screws and boards in bags and boxes.

But... surprise! The largest piece of furniture, the dining table, arrived without the instruction manual. Picture this: twenty-seven pieces of wood scattered all over the floor, hundreds of screws, and even a couple of glass panes that no one really knew what they were for.

I could perfectly envision the final result, but I had no idea

how to transform that dreadful pile of random pieces into the home of my dreams.

Can you guess why?

Because I didn't have the instruction manual.

As writers, we often have the same problem: we tend to have a clear sense of the book we dream of writing, but we get stuck when it comes to starting it or by the time we reach the middle of our story. We have vivid images of our dear characters in our heads; we can hear dialogues resonating in our minds, <u>but we lack the *instruction manual* to put it all together.</u>

Returning to my dining table story—When they finally sent me the instruction manual, I was able to assemble everything quickly and turn a lifeless, empty space into the heart of my home; similarly, **when you finish reading this book, you'll have a very clear idea of the steps to follow to plan and write your story from beginning to end.**

These pages bring together everything I've learned throughout my life about plots and narrative structure, combined with my own insights, and I'll explain it all to you in a concise and very easy-to-apply manner.

Is this book *only* for writing novels?

The answer is NO.

The main purpose of this book is to teach you how to structure and produce stories systematically, quickly, and easily. What I'm going to share with you in this manual will be helpful for writing novels, but you could apply it to many other things, such as:

- Writing short stories,
- Sharing anecdotes with your friends,
- And, in general, whenever you need to tell anything to anyone so it captures the audience's attention and keeps them listening until the end.

With a little skill, the guidelines I'm going to give you could help in many other situations: for example, in order to write the plot of a movie script or a theater play, or whenever you need to effectively structure an email newsletter for your readers, where you might want to weave together a paid offer with an engaging story from your own life.

You probably know some people who can tell you anything, no matter how boring and ordinary—for example, how they filed their taxes—and make it sound interesting, while others could meet an alien in the bakery line and still make you yawn while explaining it. The first person knows how to structure a story well and maintain suspense. The second one doesn't. My goal is to help you understand the difference between the two of them so that, no matter what you're talking about, you always know how to make it interesting to your audience.

The structure of a novel, the reader's experience, and excuses from those who don't want to study

"The structure of a novel plays a fundamental role in the reader's experience. It's important to create a clear structure that organizes the narrative elements harmoniously so that the reader remains immersed in the story..."

[Insert a yawn here.]

This was a really boring way to start, wasn't it?

"Hold on a minute. I see someone raised their hand in the back. Yes, you, the one in the polka-dot shirt. Did you want to share something with the class?"

"Excuse me, teacher, but what you're saying doesn't make sense. We can't use the same structure for all stories. They would seem like clones, like they were made with cookie cutters. They'd all be the same..."

[A murmur rises in the back. Two more students raise their hands and join the protests of the first.]

"Rules are meant to be broken, teacher!

We're artists for a reason... art is free, art flows... Art should not be confined!"

"A story needs to surprise the reader, keep them in suspense; it can't follow rules or a structure..."

Alright, let me explain this better before we continue.

We can agree that a writer is a storyteller and an artist. However, all artists, whether they're singers, painters, or sculptors, need to learn the basics of their craft before practicing it. For example, a painter needs to understand perspective, geometry, and the theory of light and shadows, while a musician needs to master singing, music theory, and the actual piano keys.

It's a well-known fact in all facets of art that, to break the rules masterfully, one must first learn them.

This book will provide you with guidelines, and your job will be to understand them so you can consciously choose when to deviate from them.

The central premise of this book is that most stories follow a pattern, and readers find comfort in the predictability of events. If you deviate too much from it, they become confused or even upset. Sometimes, they even stop reading the book because they either get bored, or they're not getting what they expected.

Humans like surprises, but in moderation, there are certain things we don't want to change. For example, we enjoy the certainty that the sun will rise in the morning and set at the end of the day. If this were to suddenly stop happening, we would feel disoriented, scared, and lost. We like the assurance that our partner will come home after work or notify us if they can't. We prefer our dog to do its business in the park rather than surprising us by doing it on the kitchen floor. Life has some pleasant surprises... and then there are *surprises* we'd rather not have.

The same goes for stories: surprises are fine... but with conditions.

Let's look at an example:

Imagine you start watching a two-hour-long detective movie, and the leading investigator (Michael) dies in a shootout twenty minutes into the film.

Now, envision two possible continuations:

- **Option a)** After Michael's funeral, his assistant continues with the case. Michael is never mentioned again in the next 100 minutes. In the end, it's the assistant (who didn't even appear until the twentieth minute) who catches the killer. Michael was just an inconsequential, unimportant collateral victim to the story. *How would you feel?*

- **Option b)** After Michael's murder, the story jumps back in time, showing us how and why the killer shot him at the twentieth minute. We discover that they went to high school together and had several conflicts there. By the end of the movie, we understand why Michael was involved in the case and why he was killed. The circle is closed. We realize why this detective was shown in action during the early minutes of the film, even though it's his assistant who ultimately solves the case.

<u>What has happened here?</u>

In example a), we feel cheated. The movie director didn't fulfill their pact with the audience. At the beginning of the plot, they promised us a story about a certain detective, made us get acquainted with him, and then got rid of him at the twenty-minute mark without even mentioning him again. In doing so, the director broke the implicit rules of storytelling, and unless they did it masterfully, it's very likely that their movie would end up a resounding failure.

In example b), all the movie director did was tell a story with a standard plot but changed the order a bit. They started the story in the middle, revealed the ending (the detective's death), and made us wait to uncover the beginning (how he met the killer and why the killer wanted to murder him). The screenwriter broke the rules but still respected the basic structure conventions. They surprised the viewer with a change, but this change didn't disrupt the structure and didn't make the audience feel deceived.

In a good story, events unfold logically and gradually, generating tension and anticipation at each stage of the narrative. Turning points are often strategically placed, typically in the same spots. You might think this is a bad idea and it will reduce the originality of your story, but it's actually a simple—and ancient—trick that helps maintain the reader's interest and excitement. A well-woven plot encourages the audience to want to find out what happens next.

Additionally, **a good plot structure allows characters to evolve significantly throughout the story, providing them with development arcs that make them seem real, human, relatable, and, overall, much more interesting than they would otherwise appear.**

In the example about our detective movie, the audience needed to know the story of Michael, the murdered investigator, and how he reached the point where someone decided to kill him. After empathizing with him during the first twenty minutes, the watchers desperately wanted to know about the character's past and the high points of his story. And if the screenwriter denies them that information, everyone will leave the theater very, very angry... and probably before the words "THE END" appear on the screen.

This is just one example of how a coherent narrative structure is essential for creating a satisfying reading experience. It doesn't matter if you're a *plotter* or a *pantser*: at the end of the day, there are only entertaining stories and monumental bore-fests. Some people have read so much that they can reproduce a standard plot without thinking, even though they're likely planning the story, albeit subconsciously. These are the famous *pantsers* and the secret why their novels don't remain unfinished or leave the reader with a sense of emptiness and "something's missing."

Now the choice is yours:

Are you going to write script a) or script b)?

Since you've purchased this book, I assume you're willing to at least give my method for planning and writing stories a chance. For that, I congratulate you... (and thank you).

Even the girl in the polka-dot shirt, the one sitting in the back who raised her hand at the beginning of the chapter, will be able to glean something useful from this reading.

Keep reading, and you'll understand why.

Write your novel using the *Autorissimo* method.

There are many methods for writing a novel, but I propose a straightforward, fast, and step-by-step approach. I'll provide you with tables and examples, and you'll see that this book's system has some features that make it different:

- **Character-plot synergy:** we'll strive to integrate the character's evolution with that of the plot. In other words, actions will unfold in harmony with the character's development. We'll use a holistic approach that addresses both the emotional aspects of the protagonist and the story's plot (what we'll later call "CHRYSALIS plot").

- **Flexible structure:** I offer you an instruction manual but also the freedom to suit your style and story. The structure I propose is highly versatile and will serve you well for writing most literary genres. I'll show you examples from a wide range of books and movies to demonstrate it in practice.

- **Evolutionary development:** we'll work on the coherent and believable evolution of characters, from their introduction to their resolution, and we'll learn to create character arcs (what we'll later refer to as *Narrative Metamorphosis* or *Character Metamorphosis*).

- **Impactful resolution:** we'll aim to conclude all stories with an emotionally resonant and satisfying resolution for the reader. Additionally, we'll work on underlying messages to add more layers of depth to the story.

What is this method about?

What I've just told you might have sounded very theoretical and confusing. But I promise that from now on, everything you read here will be self-explanatory and, above all, **helpful**.

I'm not interested in theory either; I just want a straightforward instruction manual, as I already told you. I get bored easily. I like clear instructions and examples. I already have plenty of mind-numbing books on literary theory and the craft of writing at home, and bookstores are bursting with them. Honestly, I'm aware the world doesn't need another one of those.

So, today I'm going to tell you about the system I use, which has helped me write and publish quite a few books as of today.

I named it the "Autorissimo Method," mainly because I had to call it something so we could understand each other. These are the main steps we'll follow:

- Step 1: decide that you WANT to write a story (this is more important than it seems, but if you've bought this book, we can probably skip this step).
- Step 2: Figure out the predominant GENRE of your story and its main traits.
- Step 3: Decide on the central CONFLICT.
- Step 4: Get to know the CHARACTERS and their MOTIVATIONS.

- Step 5: Describe the SETTING.
- Step 6: Learn to write a good SYNOPSIS (we'll see why).
- Step 7: Create the *skeleton* of your story with the CHRYSALIS plot.
- Step 8: Infuse your story with additional meaning by adding THEMES AND UNDERLYING MESSAGES.
- Step 9: Type until your fingers fall off (optional step). You can also use a pen or dictate into your phone.

Are you still interested?

If so, keep reading because I have **a lot** to tell you...

Who am I to tell you all of this?

Hello, my name is Eva, and I am a writer.

To this day, I've published over thirty titles—some as Eva Alton, some under a few other pen-names (or seventy-something, if we include translations and a few traditionally published books). Apart from that, I've also helped dozens of authors finish, edit, and publish their own works. I've been a beta reader for many published authors and also worked as an editor and translator.

But I'm not an English literature professor, a linguistics graduate, or, by any means, a famous author (though I'm not interested in being either). I'm just another writer, but one who once left her 9-to-5 job to pursue writing full-time.

Before becoming an author, I was an architect, so I suppose the art of planning and building things became ingrained in my soul after years of training. For those who may wonder, architects are those creatures in white helmets who sometimes wander around construction sites, tripping over tools. We usually trip over them because we are staring at a blueprint (they're not blue, by the way).

Being a writer is much safer than being an architect because you don't need to walk along the edge of an excavation pit while reading your notes. But you still need a blueprint if you don't want the work of several weeks to crumble due to a minor structural error.

Just like an architect, a writer must know what their goal is and learn how to finish things properly. When I say *things*, I mean houses, but it could also mean *books*.

Writing has always been my calling since I can remember. And as soon as I discovered that it was possible to make a living doing it, I jumped in headfirst.

I also realized that I was good at explaining things to people, and I enjoyed it. Fellow writers would contact me to ask how to do this or that, and I realized that, in my over ten years as a professional author, I had learned many things worth sharing.

So, if your goal is to finish your book and have people read it—two things that, trust me, are easier said than done, you may be interested in reading this book carefully.

Over ten years ago, I self-published my first book. Confession: it was terribly bad, and thank goodness it's not even available for sale anymore. However, that resounding failure taught me a lot. I discovered what needed to be done and, more importantly, *what shouldn't be done.* At least I finished my story, which was no small feat for a first attempt.

And I learned the following lesson as well:

> **"**
>
> *If you want to be a successful author, the first rule in this business is: learn from your mistakes and never, never, NEVER give up.*

One day, a couple of years later, the Universe gifted me with four weeks of vacation. *Four. Whole. Weeks*! I could have used them for anything (for example, going somewhere warmer or binge-watching Netflix), but instead, I decided to use them to write the first draft of a book I'd had in mind for a long time. And, *oh miracle*, this book did much better than the first one.

But... was it a miracle?

Or was it the experience gained from my mistakes with the first one?

I'll let the readers judge for themselves.

I believe it was a bit of both, but that's beside the point. The important thing is that over all these years, I've learned a lot about writing through reading, doing, talking to other authors, writing, publishing, and promoting my own and others' books. I've dealt with publishers, created promotional campaigns, laughed and cried over reader reviews, and analyzed movies and novels endlessly.

And now I'm here to share all of that with you if you so wish.

All you have to do is keep reading...

Ready?

Pen, paper...

Let's begin!

C HAPTER O NE

THE IMPORTANCE OF PLANNING

"

"If I had six hours to chop down a tree, I'd spend the first four sharpening the axe."

— Abraham Lincoln

Why plan a novel before writing it?

I know you got this book because you wanted to write a novel, and you want to start right away, but there's one thing we need to do before you begin hammering at your keyboard.

We'll start with a few exercises and reflections, so the process is quicker and easier when you actually sit down to write.

Properly planning the story, characters, and setting is crucial if you want to meet your readers' expectations. In addition to that, this prior organization has quite a few additional advantages, such as:

- You'll improve your productivity and writing speed.
- You'll enhance the intrigue and depth of the story.

- If you're writing a series, it will be much easier, and they will gain in cohesion.

Planning and Productivity

I'm sure you've heard of some writers who publish a deluge of titles each year. How do they do it? What's their trick? Maybe they can type really fast? *Newsflash: typing lighting fast is by no means the best-kept secret of prolific writers.* Not at all! There are other much more influential factors, such as consistency, routine, and taking care of physical and mental health. But in my opinion, **the most important one is knowing what you're going to write before starting each writing session**. If you don't know what you're supposed to do, you're very likely to end up staring at the wall or writing lines you'll later erase.

If you don't have a blueprint or a map, you'll almost certainly end up getting lost... or wasting precious time.

> *"The most important factor in writing quickly and well is knowing what you're going to write before you start each writing session."*

Planning and Suspense in Stories

A well-planned plot will help you avoid narrative pitfalls, such as forced twists or inconsistencies in the story's internal logic. If you know what's going to happen before it happens, you can avoid contradictions and ensure a smoother reading experience. Moreover, you can drop hints that increase intrigue and create anticipation in the reader as they progress toward the story's conclusion.

Sure, you can write everything in one go and go back a thousand times to add and remove things, but that will make you lose more time, force you to rewrite entire chapters, and may lead to forgetting lots of things and making more mistakes than necessary. You might even become frustrated and give up halfway.

Besides that, having an overview of the whole story will help you understand the central theme of the narrative and make exploring underlying messages easier: you will be able to weave layers of meaning throughout the story as you write it. As the saying goes, ***"Sometimes the trees don't let us see the forest."*** When we plan a novel in advance, we see the entire forest; when we write blindly, we only see small branches, and they might obstruct our overall view.

Planning and Cohesion

It doesn't matter whether you're writing fiction or non-fiction: knowing what you're going to write in each section/scene/chapter will prevent repetition and ensure you don't forget any key points. If you're writing a fiction series, meticulous planning becomes even more crucial. Imagine getting to the last book in a trilogy and realizing you can't resolve the ending as you wanted because you'd have to change a vital fact in the first book... *which is already published!*

But... do I really have to plan everything before starting?

Of course not!

You can always improvise whenever you want or need to.

I'm going to provide you with some tracks to help you move forward more quickly, but it's entirely normal to veer off them and improvise. Don't take these as unbreakable rules; they're just tools to prevent writer's block while you get your story off your chest.

The purpose of this book is to make you reflect, ask yourself questions, and help you refine that vague novel idea that has been lingering in your head for ages. It'll help you make it tangible, clear, and more manageable.

This book includes tables, exercises, and questions, but that doesn't mean you have to fill them all out or have answers ready for all the questions posed. Leaving blank gaps is okay. Discovering your characters' traits or resolving specific conflicts later, as you write, is completely normal and expected.

In fact, I encourage you to complete all the exercises **in pencil** and have an eraser on hand.

Whether you're a natural planner or more of a discovery writer, finding clarity will help you write better and faster, whether you're more like Hansel or Gretel...

And while we're on the subject of those two poor fictional children who got lost in the woods, let's move on to the next point.

Pantsers, Plotters, and How *Not* to End Up Like Hansel and Gretel

Once upon a time, there were two writers named Hansel and Gretel. Hansel was analytical and methodical, while Gretel was a free spirit who liked to go with the flow. One day, they got lost in a forest of revisions, and it didn't take much for them to come close to being devoured by a ruthless creature named...

...Writer's Block.

When I started writing, I didn't know any other authors, so I was unfamiliar with the concepts of "pantser" and "plotter." I just knew that I had to sit down and type until I reached the end of my book, and that was all.

But later, I found out that everyone has their own writing style, all valid and useful. In my story, I'll call the two main types of writers Hansel and Gretel, even though they're mostly referred to as pantsers and plotters.

A "pantser," or a discovery writer, is someone who dives into the story without a fixed plan, letting the characters and plot evolve organically as they write. This writer goes with their intuition and explores the twists of the story as they emerge. Note: I want to emphasize the word "intuition" here (because our intuition can be good, mediocre, or terrible, and this will determine the quality of the final result).

On the other hand, a "plotter" is someone who prefers to have a clear structure and a detailed plan before starting to write. Typically, they take notes, create outlines, develop character profiles, and carefully construct a plot before beginning to write.

Both approaches have their advantages and disadvantages, but I believe that in the literary world, we have a romanticized idea of discovery writers: they seem to wander aimlessly through the forest of creation like magical fairies, wielding a pen instead of a wand. It almost seems as if having a roadmap or a plot is akin to stripping the creative process of all its artistic value.

But is this true?

In my opinion, regardless of your preferred style, whether it's plotting or pantsing, you still have to consider the preferences of readers. And a widespread preference among readers is reading finished stories that make sense.

If Hansel and Gretel had had a map, they could have easily found their way home. Since they didn't have one, they marked the path with breadcrumbs, which is essentially a variation of the same thing.

But what if Hansel and Gretel hadn't had a map (or breadcrumbs) to guide them? Would they have had any chance of finding their way home?

The answer is *yes, as long as they had learned the way beforehand.* In that case, the map would have been in their minds. If mom had taught them the way when they were little, they wouldn't have needed a map or breadcrumbs.

If you know the way, you'll always know clearly where to turn and where to go straight, without any aids or crutches. Think of when you go to work in the mornings: do you ever get there and feel like you were driving your car on autopilot? You didn't need a GPS, let alone a street map. You just parked in front of the building, and you couldn't even remember how you got there because the process was so internalized that you weren't even paying attention.

This is the exact same thing that happens to writers.

When you write, you can follow your intuition (your inner

compass), or you can create an outline and follow it just like a baking recipe. Both methods can be effective and yield brilliant results. But what no one usually tells us is that the *"let's see what comes out"* strategy tends to be much more successful if:

a) You're an experienced writer, and you already know the way by heart.
b) You've read so many novels that you know the general structure of a story subconsciously.
c) You're a genius (like Stephen King or Agatha Christie, for example).

The first two options are almost the same: in both cases, we're talking about people who have an internal GPS fueled by experience. They can go with the flow because their intuition tells them when it's necessary to take a turn in the story. The third is a rare occurrence, and for simplicity's sake, I'll assume that none of us belongs to the genius group.

In my opinion, all pantser writers had to learn the correct structuring of a story at some point in their lives. Perhaps they learned it subconsciously, even as children, while reading, watching movies, or listening to bedtime stories their mother made up every night. But 99.99% of them acquired that skill, even if they don't remember how or when.

Therefore, my dear fellow authors, I believe that it's beneficial for all of us to read writing craft books from time to time, regardless of what type of author we are.

We can mark the way with breadcrumbs, like Hansel, or we can close our eyes and embark on the adventure, like Gretel. But if we want to reach the goal (that is, a coherent and *finished* novel), it will be advantageous to know where we are going and the quickest route to get there.

Consider this book your breadcrumbs: I hope these pages save you from an unfinished story and help you avoid a few inconsistencies. If you're a pantser, this manual will help nourish your internal GPS. If you're a plotter, you'll surely enjoy the worksheets and diagrams included.

Now you know what this book is about, let's move forward.

We're going to break down our loaf of bread, starting at the first turn on the road.

Today's task: step 1

Today, I only ask that you get a notebook to complete the exercises from the following chapters.

You can also get the workbook that complements this book: "*Practical Workbook: How to Write a Novel Step-by-Step,*" part of the *Autorissimo* collection. It includes worksheets and templates to plan characters, develop your plot, and much more. Check it out at this link:

mybook.to/noveloutlining

But don't worry; it's not essential. Any notebook will do. However, I recommend that you don't use a digital application, as writing by hand activates certain parts of the brain connected to creativity.

Also, avoid loose sheets of paper, as they might end up getting mixed up or lost.

C HAPTER T WO

Find your genre

"

"If you don't know where you are going, you will probably end up somewhere else."

~ Lawrence J. Peter

Once upon a time, there was a young shepherd named Santiago who dreamed of a treasure. This dream haunted him until he could take it no longer. So, he left everything behind and embarked on an arduous journey to find the treasure.

I wish I could say that I made up this story myself, but I'm actually thinking about *The Alchemist* by Paulo Coelho. Santiago, the protagonist, is not very different from us writers: in the end, we all dream of finding a treasure—it doesn't always have to be a chest of gold; it can also be a literary success in any form.

If you've read the book, you'll know that Santiago found his treasure at the end. *The Alchemist* is filled with valuable lessons, but today, I want to focus on <u>one of the main reasons why the protagonist found what he was looking for</u> so you can copy his strategy and use it, too. After all, starting a novel is not much

31

different from embarking on a journey: we know there will be obstacles, surprises, and fellow travelers, some wonderful and others not so much.

Luckily, Santiago's secret was very simple: he found his treasure because he had _a clear goal_. Santiago knew where he was going... he had <u>the ending</u> in mind.

What about you? Do you know the ending of your novel? Do you know its genre, who the protagonist will be, and what the key points of the story will be? Do you know who the antagonist is and why they did what they did? Or do you perceive your book as a nebulous sensation or a couple of disjointed images floating around your brain? If you answered with the second option, keep reading because the following chapters are designed to turn those floating fragments of stories into a solid foundation to begin building upon. That way, you'll not only know that you want to go on vacation, but you'll also know whether you need to pack for Morocco or Iceland... and dress accordingly.

What are literary genres, and how can they be useful?

Literary genres are categories under which we group literary works that share similar characteristics.

When a reader enters a bookstore (or an online store), they usually head to the section where their favorite genre is located: it's the easiest and quickest way to find books they like.

Books of the same genre tend to be similar in terms of style, theme, narrative structure, and lots of other things. Readers go to a particular section of their bookstore because they know, thanks to their previous experience, that they'll find something they like there.

When planning your story, it's essential to decide which genre it belongs to because each one adheres to certain conventions, and if you disregard them, readers will be puzzled and probably unsatisfied.

This may seem like a straightforward step, but many people forget about it and start writing their story without considering the genre and subgenres. In the worst case, neglecting this small detail can make the novel unsellable. For example, if you decide to write a romance novel, create a cover that shows two people kissing and a title or subtitle that talks about love, readers will expect the central plot to revolve around a couple falling in love, overcoming the obstacles that kept them apart, and ultimately finding their happy ending. If this doesn't happen in your book, many readers will be disappointed and won't recommend your book to their friends (that is, they'll leave you terrible reviews).

So, can I deviate from genres or mix them?

Yes, of course, you can. Many literary masters have done so with great success, and they continue to do so. But we need to start with the ABCs and 123s. Equations with derivatives and integrals will come later.

The most popular literary genres

Let's take a quick look at the literary genres that you usually find in most bookstores so you can make sure your story belongs to the genre you think it does. Of course, this classification is fluid, and there are mixed genres where elements of different stories are combined. However, it will serve as a general overview and help you decide on the main genre of your story.

- **Romance**: This is one of the best-selling genres (according to some sources, *the* best-selling, although it competes with crime and mystery novels). In any case, all romance novels have a common denominator: exploring interpersonal relationships and offering a happy ending to the reader. Most stories of any genre include a romantic subplot because love is a universal human theme. Romance encompasses love stories of all kinds, with subgenres dividing it by time period, age of the reader or protagonist, sexual identity of the characters, tone of the novel (from dramatic to romantic comedy), fantastic or realistic setting, etc. Some popular romance subgenres are:
  - Romantic comedy: this subgenre includes humorous situations, such as *Bridget Jones's Diary* by Helen Fielding.
  - Historical romances: these are novels set in the past. It has many subgenres depending on the historical period, e.g., Regency, medieval, Greco-

Roman, etc. A well-known example is *Outlander* by Diana Gabaldon, set in 18th-century Scotland.

- o Fantasy romance: in these stories, the romantic relationship takes place in a fantasy world or between supernatural characters (wizards, vampires, werewolves, fairies, etc.). Example: *From Blood and Ash* by Jennifer L. Armentrout.

- o Erotic romance: these are romance novels that include explicit content, such as *Fifty Shades of Grey* by E.L. James. Note: a purely erotic story without a romantic relationship (by this, I mean the characters must fall in love) is not technically a romance novel. A romance novel needs characters who fall in love, and a happy ending is usually expected.

- **Crime or detective fiction**: this genre focuses on intrigue and solving a crime or mystery. These novels are characterized by suspense and the ability to keep the reader in tension until the central conflict is resolved, often in a surprising way. For example:

  - o Police procedural novels: the action centers on police investigation and the procedures followed to solve a crime. For example, *The Silence of the Lambs* by Thomas Harris.

  - o *Noir* fiction: similar to detective novels but often offers a darker atmosphere and explores the complexity of the human mind and its darker aspects, such as internal conflicts, past traumas, or ethical dilemmas. Example: *The Girl with the Dragon Tattoo* by Stieg Larsson.

- ○ Psychological thriller: like all thrillers, there is usually a crime or mystery to solve, but the novel focuses on the minds and motivations of the characters. For example, *The Girl on the Train* by Paula Hawkins.

- **Science Fiction:** In this genre, you often find scientific and technological elements, which can be real or fictional. Futurism and settings in other worlds or galaxies are also common, usually in a way that seems plausible to the reader. Often, these novels include a background of social criticism and speculate on the impact of technological advances and their ethical and moral implications.

  - ○ Space operas: adventures and explorations in outer space, like *Star Wars* by George Lucas.

  - ○ Dystopian novels: these explore future societies, usually oppressive and dehumanized, like *1984* by George Orwell and *The Handmaid's Tale* by Margaret Atwood.

  - ○ Time travel: novels where the protagonists travel to the past or the future. These stories examine time travel adventures and their repercussions. For example, *The Time Machine* by H.G. Wells.

  - ○ Steampunk: these novels combine fantasy elements with a distinctive *Steampunk* look that includes aspects of the Victorian era and complex steam-powered machinery with gears.

- **Fantasy**: Fantasy novels take place in worlds that can be entirely imaginary or similar to the real world but include magical and fantastical elements. The main characters often have magical or supernatural powers. Like the other genres, fantasy has many subgenres, such as:
    - High fantasy or epic fantasy, with highly detailed imaginary worlds. For example, *The Lord of the Rings* by J.R.R. Tolkien.
    - Urban fantasy: the story is set in a contemporary urban environment populated with supernatural beings. For example, *City of Bones* by Cassandra Clare.
    - Dark fantasy: this subgenre often deals with darker themes, and the line between good and evil ("the good guys" and "the bad guys") is not as straightforward as in others. An example is *The Name of the Wind* by Patrick Rothfuss.
- **Horror**: This type of fiction aims to provoke fear or startle the reader and maintain suspense throughout the book. It has many subgenres, for example:
    - Supernatural horror: includes supernatural or monstrous creatures, such as ghosts, zombies, or demons. For example, *Dracula* by Bram Stoker.
    - Psychological horror: this type of novel tries to terrorize the reader through psychological and

mental elements or through what happens in the character's mind. It relies on suspense and tension rather than using supernatural monsters or gory scenes. Example: *The Shining* by Stephen King.

- o Gothic horror: this genre often has a gothic, macabre, and gloomy setting, such as ruined castles or cemeteries.

Apart from these, there are many other literary genres and subgenres, such as contemporary literature, women's fiction, travel fiction, young adult literature, etc., besides all the subgenres of non-fiction. All in all, there are too many to mention each one in this book, and the list seems to grow day by day. If you write in any of these, don't worry: they are only examples, and you can do further research on your own, as we will see in the following pages.

Today's task: step 2

To complete today's task, you'll need a notebook.

- Make a list of a few books you have enjoyed. What do they have in common?
- Turn on the television and check the latest programs you've watched. Pay special attention to the series and movies you usually watch. Do you see any common patterns? What genres does the app recommend to you?

Based on your notes, try to answer these questions:

- What is your favorite genre (or genres)?
- Would you like to write a novel/story in this genre?
- Can you come up with ideas for similar stories to those books and movies but with new and original elements added by you?

Over the next few weeks:

- Try to watch at least three movies or series in the genre (or genres) you like the most, and write down the plot of each story in your notebook.
- Read at least three books from your chosen genre and take notes.

- Write down the titles.
- Note the genre (if you're unsure, an internet search can help. You can search, for example, "What genre does *The Lord of the Rings* belong to?").
- Describe the cover image.
- Write a summary of the plot.
- Note who the protagonist is.
- Describe why you liked it.
- Note if there are any farfetched or boring parts.

Considering your previous answers, **think about possible changes and improvements** you would add to make each story better or different.

This task may take some time, depending on your reading/watching speed, but it's an integral part of the process. If you've already read several books in your favorite genre and still remember them, you can use those for this exercise. In the upcoming chapters, we will revisit these movies and books and analyze them in greater depth.

CHAPTER THREE

The secret sauce

"

"Life is either a daring adventure or nothing at all."
—Helen Keller

I've always had a deep admiration for Helen Keller. I read her biography many years ago and was captivated by her courage and determination. Helen Keller lost her hearing and sight at a young age, yet she became a writer and activist, which wasn't particularly easy for 19th-century women.

Helen Keller refused to lead a dull and uneventful life despite all the obstacles fate placed in her path. She realized that **we're only given one life, and if we don't do anything memorable during the few years we have, it's as if we aren't truly living.** Helen Keller's life is almost like a novel because she had to overcome seemingly insurmountable obstacles to achieve her goals, relying on her unwavering determination.

In the following pages, we'll discuss the importance of having difficulties and challenges in your story that your characters can face, just as Helen had to do in order to become the remarkable woman she was.

In the previous chapter, I asked you to reflect on the genre of your novel and research other books, movies, and TV series that are similar. My goal was for you to arrive at this point with a clear idea of the type of novel you want to write and to have thoroughly analyzed at least three examples of stories similar to yours.

Why? Because we're about to start building the basic foundations upon which we'll later construct the whole plot.

In order to do that, we need to answer the following questions, which will largely depend on the genre you have chosen:

- What happened?
- To whom?
- Where?
- How?

See why you needed to figure out the right genre first?

Note: Don't worry if you can't answer these questions right now. The aim of the upcoming chapters is to help you clarify these key points and find several answers. In the following pages, I'll assist you with examples and ideas and provide exercises to make your ideas more tangible.

In this chapter, The Secret Sauce, we're going to begin with the WHAT of the story, and then we'll continue with the rest of the questions.

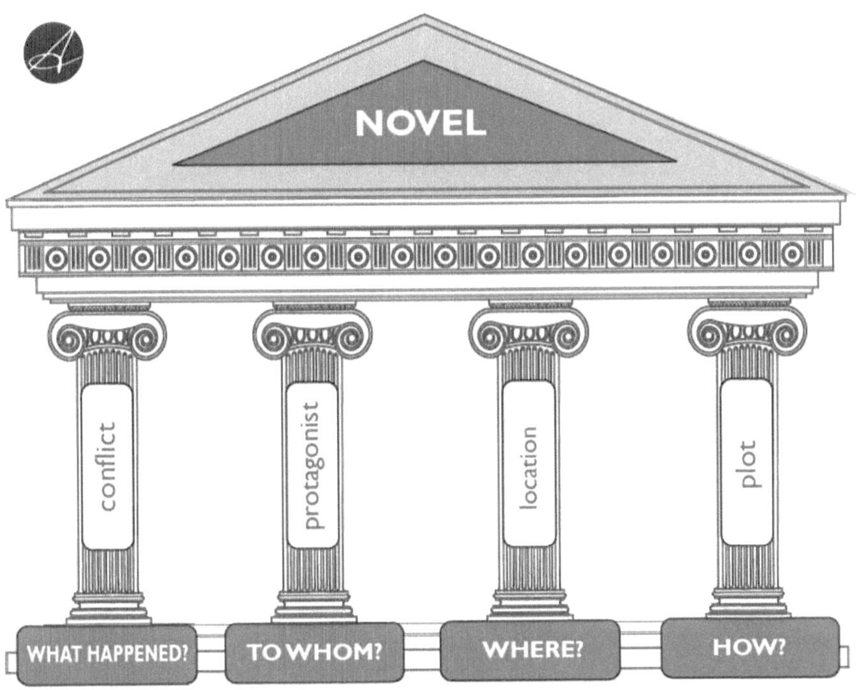

The pillars of a story

WHAT HAPPENS IN THE STORY?

Or, in other words:

What problem must your protagonist solve?

That is:

What is the MAIN CONFLICT?

Yes! There's a magical ingredient that distinguishes a good story from a boring or mediocre one, and this secret ingredient is called...

CONFLICT.

Every good writer knows that without conflict, there is no story. Imagine if Romeo and Juliet had fallen in love, and their families had said, *"Sure, you can get married. Who cares about our family feuds? Long live love!"* It would have been very nice and all, but it would have also been a very short (and very boring) story. I doubt its fame would have lasted for four centuries. The magic of Romeo and Juliet is suffering with them for their impossible love; turning the pages while biting your nails, wondering if there's a way for a Montague and a Capulet to be happily together, feeling your heart break when Romeo poisons himself due to a misunderstanding, believing Juliet is dead, and even more when she wakes up a little while later, finding her beloved lying lifeless next to her...

That's the kind of story that moves the readers: the one that makes them suffer or fall in love when they step into the character's shoes. The one that makes them feel hatred, sadness, or anger or burst into incontrollable laughter. The one that reminds them that, even though their life is the same every day and perhaps a bit dull, they're still alive and capable of feeling strong emotions deep in their soul.

That's the key.

That's *The Secret Sauce.*

<u>A good story must make us feel something.</u>

And in order for that to happen, protagonists must struggle. If everything in their life were easy, their story would leave us completely indifferent.

The *WHAT*, or the conflict, is the central problem that the protagonist must solve. A good conflict is the engine of the plot and the driving force that keeps readers or viewers hooked. If you don't have a clear and well-developed conflict, your story will lack tension and excitement.

The *WHAT*, or the conflict, is the central problem

that the protagonist must solve.

Remember: your characters' lives can't be easy. If everything goes perfectly for them from the start, the reader will start yawning, turn off the light, and go to sleep. Our diabolical goal is to keep them glued to the page with their eyes wide open so that the next day, they arrive at work exhausted because they couldn't put down your book until four in the morning.

Even when you're telling an anecdote from your daily life to your friends, it's crucial to make the conflict of your story clear right from the get-go. This way, you can create intrigue as the audience wonders how you managed to get out of that challenging situation.

For example:

- I took a train to go to an amusement park a hundred miles from my city, and when I arrived there, I realized I had forgotten my wallet...

- Right after coming back from the notary's office, where I had just signed the mortgage for my house, I sat down in the office and found a termination letter on the table...

- My girlfriend's parents invited me to lunch, and when I saw the cars parked outside, I realized they had also invited my secret lover...

Are you curious to find out how these stories ended? I bet you are! And do you know why? Because the protagonist just got into a tremendous mess.

In a novel, it's even easier to establish what the central conflict is, as this is often dictated by the predominant genre. That's why I asked you to first research which genre your story belongs to. Each genre has its own characteristics and conventions, and in the following examples, we'll explore some of them so that you can see how to use genres to determine the WHAT of your own story.

Thriller:

Conflict: The protagonist is thrust into a situation of extreme danger and must fight for their life or confront a deadly threat.

Examples:

- *The Da Vinci Code* by Dan Brown. Symbolism professor Robert Langdon becomes embroiled in a religious conspiracy and is accused of a murder he didn't commit. He must decipher codes and clues to unravel a hidden truth and save himself.
- *Vertigo*, a film directed by Alfred Hitchcock. A retired detective becomes obsessed with the mystery of a deceased woman and finds himself ensnared in a web of deception and betrayals that he must unravel if he wants to survive.

Mystery and Detective Novels:

Conflict: A crime has occurred, and the protagonist, often a detective or investigator, must solve the mystery and uncover who is responsible for the crime. To do so, they must gather clues, interrogate suspects, analyze evidence, and overcome obstacles until they unravel the hidden truth behind the crime and discover the culprit and their motive.

Examples:

- *The Silence of the Lambs* by Thomas Harris. Clarice Starling, an FBI agent, delves into the mind of a dangerous serial killer named Hannibal Lecter while trying to solve a brutal series of homicides.
- *Murder on the Orient Express* by Agatha Christie. Detective Hercule Poirot investigates the murder of a passenger on the luxurious Orient Express train, where all the occupants seem to be suspects.

Romance:

Conflict: Two people fall in love, but obstacles are preventing them from being together. Adversity will test their love, and they must overcome differences, external conflicts, or social barriers to achieve their desired happy ending.

Examples:

- *Wuthering Heights* by Emily Brontë: In this novel, Catherine Earnshaw passionately loves Heathcliff, whom she has known since childhood, but she marries Edgar Linton for social status and wealth. Catherine is torn between her desire for a life of luxury and her love for Heathcliff.

- In the movie, *Pretty Woman*, a prostitute and a wealthy businessman are attracted to each other, but they must face social barriers and deep differences that separate them if they want their relationship to thrive.

Fantasy:

Conflict: There are many subgenres of fantasy, but often, the main problem revolves around the forces of evil threatening a fantasy world. The protagonist must embark on an epic adventure to save their world or their people, facing magical creatures, dark forces, or a prophecy.

Examples:

- *The Lord of the Rings* by J.R.R. Tolkien: Frodo Baggins, a hobbit accustomed to a comfortable and peaceful life, must destroy an evil ring to prevent it from falling into the hands of the Dark Lord, Sauron. If Sauron were to obtain the One Ring, he would become invincible and could subdue all the free peoples of Middle-earth.
- *Harry Potter and the Philosopher's Stone* by J.K. Rowling: Harry Potter, an orphaned boy, is invited to a school of magic and must confront the Dark Lord, Voldemort, if he wishes to preserve his life and prevent the Dark Lord

from becoming the ruler of the magical world, sowing terror and destruction.

Science Fiction:

Conflict: The story is set in a dystopian future or in a scenario of scientific advancements where the protagonist must fight against oppression, explore new worlds, or confront ethical dilemmas, depending on the subgenre.

Examples:

- *1984* by George Orwell: Winston Smith defies the totalitarian government of a dystopian society, trying to prevent The Party from eliminating all free-thinking human beings.
- In the movie, *The Matrix*, a young hacker named Neo discovers that the reality he lives in is a simulation created by intelligent machines to keep humanity under control. Neo must confront the machines to free humanity from the grip of the Matrix.

Today's task: step 3

In this chapter, we have seen a few examples of conflict classified by genre. If you completed the exercise from the previous chapter (reading three books, watching three movies, etc.), now is the time to analyze the stories you chose and jot down in your notebook what the main conflict is for each one. Try to summarize the central problem as we did in the examples on the previous pages.

Create a table for each title, including:

- Title of the story
- Genre it belongs to
- Main conflict

 CONFLICT WORKSHEET

TITLE:

GENRE:

MAIN CONFLICT:

C H A P T E R F O U R

When Characters Come to Life

> **"The two most important days in your life are the day you are born and the day you find out why."**
>
> — Mark Twain

THE *WHO* OF YOUR STORY

Perfect: you already have a story and, above all, a serious problem that needs to be solved. But... who will take care of solving everything? In other words:

Who is the protagonist of your book?

A novel without characters would be as intriguing as a school physics book: an endless exposition of facts that don't happen to anyone in particular and that don't provoke any emotion in the reader.

But to captivate the reader, it will take much more than making up just any character who experiences things.

Our protagonists will need to be proactive, and above all, they must have something that drives them, something that keeps them moving forward. This **something** is called...

MOTIVATION.

If I had to choose a single word that summarizes the essence of this book and of any worthwhile novel, I would probably choose that one.

Motivation, yes.

Or perhaps *metamorphosis*, but we'll talk about that later.

I don't care if your protagonist is blond, tall, or has thirteen tentacles. I don't care if they live in a straw house or on a satellite orbiting the Milky Way.

What does matter a lot to me, and to your readers, is this character's irresistible desire to achieve something. What drives them to do what they do? What is it that compels them to keep fighting... *and me to keep reading?*

Many novice writers spend hours and hours deciding the exact number of freckles on their protagonist's nose, but they forget to give them a deep ambition, a longing, or a driving force that urges them to move forward. That's one of the worst mistakes we can make, and if not resolved, it will lead you to write a dull novel, more soporific than two cups of concentrated chamomile tea. But hey, you'll have a handsome protagonist.

Let's take a moment to reflect on the main character (or

characters) of your story. The goal is that, when you finish this book, you can visualize them and have conversations with them in your head (don't worry, all writers do it, and it's not a cause for concern... by itself). Having a clear vision of your characters will make their behavior consistent and, above all, <u>believable</u> throughout the story.

MOTIVATION is the strong desire that drives the main character of a story to achieve something.

We'll start with some examples of motivation and then go over several key points you should consider when creating your characters. Finally, we'll work together to create a character profile for your protagonist.

The character arc and *Character Metamorphosis*

In a good story, the protagonist must undergo a significant change as the plot unfolds. This change can be personal growth, emotional transformation, or a significant learning experience.

> ### *CHARACTER METAMORPHOSIS*
>
> *"A process in which we describe how the protagonist of a story undergoes an internal transformation that impacts how they handle challenges."*

The character arc typically goes like this: a character begins their journey because *they want something*, although *it's usually not what they truly need*. They will discover this difference later as they evolve through the trials they must face during their journey.

This is a key aspect of what I call *Character Metamorphosis:*

- First, the character WANTS SOMETHING.
- Then, they overcome various trials that teach them a lesson.
- Due to this, the character undergoes a METAMORPHOSIS or REVELATION.
- In the end, the character UNDERSTANDS WHAT THEY TRULY NEED to resolve the situation.

Character arc and character metamorphosis

During a novel, characters must resolve challenges that force them to change, learn, and reflect. If they do it right, they'll eventually realize what they truly need.

In a good story, the evolution of the main character should be closely tied to the development of the plot, as we will see later on.

Examples of Character Metamorphosis

Let's see some examples of *Character Metamorphosis:*

- *Twilight* by Stephenie Meyer: At the beginning of the story, Bella Swan is an introverted and lonely teenager who moves to the town of Forks to live with her father.

Her only desire is to adapt to her new life and go unnoticed at school. However, when she meets Edward Cullen and discovers that he is a vampire, she falls in love with him and realizes that her true longing is to be together with him despite the obstacles, to become a part of Edward's supernatural world, and to protect her family from dangers she didn't even know existed.

- o What she wants at the beginning: to go unnoticed and be invisible.
- o What she needs: to overcome situations that prevent her from enjoying her relationship with Edward.
- o How she learns it: she's forced to confront dangers she never imagined and realizes that she's stronger and braver than she thought.

- *The Picture of Dorian Gray* by Oscar Wilde: at the beginning of the story, Dorian Gray is a handsome and vain young man who desires to maintain his beauty and youth forever. His only wish is for the portrait that has been painted of him to age in his place while he retains his youthful appearance and indulges in a life of debauchery and wickedness without caring about the feelings of others. Over time and under the corrupting influence of Lord Henry, Dorian descends into a life of libertinism, where he only seeks to satisfy his selfish desires regardless of the consequences. In the end, he realizes that his true need is to find peace and redemption before the end of his life and to do so, he must face the terrible consequences of his actions.

- o What he wants at the beginning: to have fun without consequences and never grow old.
- o What he needs: to take responsibility for his actions and the harm he causes to others.
- o How he learns it: the decay of his portrait reflects his own moral corruption and wickedness.

- *Indiana Jones and the Dial of Destiny*, directed by James Mangold: at the beginning of the story, aged Indy appears as an anonymous and solitary university professor. His only desire is to retire and live alone and in peace, away from his adventurous past. Life's setbacks made him forget what he really needed and longed for, even though he denied it. He will need to overcome various trials to understand that what truly gave meaning to his life was archaeology, adventure, and having a family to love.

  - o What he wants at the beginning: a solitary, routine, and discreet life.
  - o What he needs: to rediscover adventures, his passion for archaeology, and his family.
  - o How he learns it: when he's pushed into a new adventure, he realizes what was missing in his life and how much he missed it.

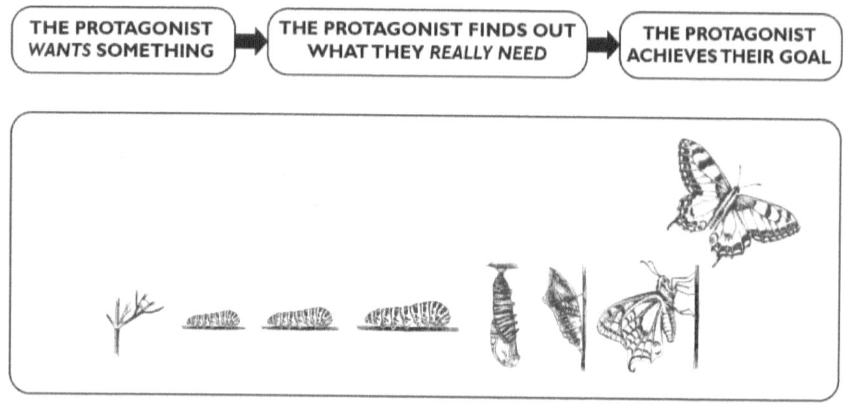

Character metamorphosis for series

If you're writing a series, you'll need to create a gradual metamorphosis. Make the changes in the protagonist noticeable but staged so that the reader can see them grow as a person little by little and enjoy small victories that will lead to the series' ultimate climax.

Although it may sound complex at first, it's not a difficult thing to do if you plan ahead. You just need to create an overarching character arc and subdivide it into smaller arcs that occur during each episode, as follows:

- <u>Metamorphosis throughout the series</u> (from Book 1 to Book 3): a substantial change that drives the main plot of the series.

- <u>Metamorphosis during each episode:</u> small changes and improvements that prepare the character for their final revelation. I recommend that the protagonist doesn't reach the "big and final revelation" in the very first book and solve all their traumas and problems all at once; this may cause many readers to abandon the series midway. Instead, have them solve a small problem during each episode and always leave some loose threads to maintain interest.

I'll illustrate this with an example using the story of Nadia, an imaginary character who is about to graduate from the fire academy. Nadia had a five-year-old son whom she left in the care of her ex-boyfriend for a few days to finish her academy exams. Her ex-boyfriend drove drunk with the child in the car, resulting in their deaths in a car accident. Since then, Nadia has suffered from post-traumatic stress and is unable to talk about the accident or trust anyone other than herself, not even for the most trivial things.

- Global Metamorphosis: at the beginning of the series, Nadia is a completely distrustful and unhappy woman due to her traumas. She has become a lonely person, friendless, and incapable of opening up to others. However, her profession as a firefighter will require her to learn to delegate tasks and entrust others with them. At the end of the series, she'll have to jump from a burning building into the arms of her best friend, showing complete faith in him and mustering the courage to declare her love for him.
  - o What she wants: to live alone and in peace, forget the past by ignoring it, not talk about her

deceased son, and focus entirely on her work.

- What she needs: to accept what happened, open up to others, rebuild her life, and learn to love again.
- How she learns: her rescue missions force her to work in a team and learn to trust others.

- Staged Metamorphosis:
  - Book 1: Nadia and her partner Raj, through joint work, manage to rescue a baby from a burning building. After this experience, she talks to him for the first time about her son's accident. Raj becomes her first friend and confidant in a long time.
  - Book 2: Nadia and Raj participate in a highly dangerous mission where a fuel depot threatens to explode and level the entire city. They emerge victorious. They start falling in love, but she's unable to express her feelings openly.
  - Book 3: Nadia finds herself in a life-or-death situation, but by this point, she has learned that there are people she can fully trust. Raj saves her from a fire in her apartment building. After this experience, she finally confesses her feelings to the man she loves. She's now ready to accept her past, understand that her son's accident was not her fault, and rebuild her life.

Physical appearance

In my humble opinion, a character's physical appearance is one of the less important aspects in planning a novel, and it's one I usually spend less time on compared to others. I believe it's not strictly necessary to spend hours and hours detailing the physical appearance of characters unless you enjoy doing it as a hobby. In most genres, it's much more helpful to spend that time detailing their personality, flaws, and motivation. In fact, sometimes, I like to leave a bit to the reader's imagination so they can add their preferred features to the protagonist and feel more connected to them.

Of course, it's essential to decide and remember the basic physical characteristics of your character to avoid them having blue eyes in Chapter 1 and brown eyes in Chapter 8. You can jot down these characteristics in a notebook or on a character sheet, look for pictures on the internet of people who resemble them, or even generate their appearance by inputting the description into an artificial intelligence tool if you don't object to using one.

In any case, try to avoid making your protagonist tall, handsome, and absolutely perfect because that can detract from their credibility and might even create envy or dislike in the reader. Instead, give them something unique and different, a minor flaw or mark that makes them more realistic and human. For example, a scar, a slouched posture, bitten nails... and while you're at it, try to tie this flaw into the rest of the story. For instance, Harry Potter wears eccentric round glasses and has a scar on his forehead that links him to Voldemort, the main villain of the story.

<u>Important</u>: Although it's useful for YOU to know your protagonist's appearance, avoid giving a lengthy description resembling a police sketch at the beginning of your novel. Save detailed character descriptions for character profiles. These kinds of descriptions are typical of beginner writers and can often be redundant and slow down the pacing of the story. Do yourself and your readers a favor and never, ever put the protagonist in front of a mirror in Chapter 1, reciting the color of their eyes, the exact thickness of their eyebrows in millimeters, and how sexy their lips look when they pronounce the letter O.

Your protagonist's personality

While your protagonist may be a human being just like everyone else, you can still try to give them a characteristic that makes them unique and memorable. They can be brave, intelligent, persistent, or possess any other quality relevant to the plot. But be careful, don't give them only positive characteristics. Above all, a good character should never be perfect, which leads us to the next point...

• **Flaws**: Flaws make a character more realistic and human. You can make them selfish, impatient, insecure, or any other trait that you can later use to develop their character, help them grow as a person, and learn valuable lessons throughout the story.

NOTE:

In the following character descriptions and profiles, I have used the term "flaws" in a simplified manner to quickly highlight the unique characteristics of each individual in the story. My intention is only to make the profile sheets shorter and more straightforward. However, I want to emphasize that each of these traits contributes to the richness and authenticity of the characters in the plot. I recognize the diversity and uniqueness of each person and their physical and emotional particularities. If you disagree with the use of this term, replace the word "flaw" in your character sheet with "distinctive personal traits."

Character Profile

PROFILE 1: ISABELLA FROM "THE MAGIC OF THE AMAZON"

(Made up Fantasy Novel I Might Write One Day)

Character Name: Isabella Duarte, sometimes goes by the alias Isobel James.

Age: 30 years (during the novel, set in 2022)

Date of Birth: August 15, 1992.

Profession: Street vendor (handmade jewelry).

Physical Description:

Isabella is of average height with a mane of dark, curly hair that frames her warm face and her sharp eyes. Her tanned skin and ethnic jewelry add a touch of mystery to her appearance.

Personality:

Isabella is enigmatic and open-minded, always seeking the unusual in every corner of the world. Isabella is friendly and enjoys conversing with people about their problems and desires, making her an involuntary confidante. While confident, she's also cautious and distrustful of those who try to exploit her mysterious supernatural gifts.

Flaws:

- Physical: She has a scar on her right hand that she always tries to hide. She acquired it while attempting to use her magic to save her parents, unsuccessfully, and she never wants to talk about it.
- Personality: At times, she can be too stubborn and reluctant to trust others due to her past experiences. This lack of trust gets her into trouble throughout the story until she overcomes it.

Distinctive Features (magical powers, rare talents, etc.):

She has the ability to communicate with animals and sense magical energy around her. She can concentrate rays of fire that shoot from her wrists by gathering energy from all nearby animals.

Background Story:

Isabella grew up in a remote village in the Amazon jungle, where her family moved under the pretext of studying the local fauna. In truth, her parents fled their hometown, where they were accused of practicing witchcraft. At a young age, she suffered the mysterious loss of her parents, which left a deep mark on her. She was adopted by an elderly native woman who tried to introduce her to the tradition of witchcraft, but she refused. Later, she decided to embark on a journey to find answers about her parents' death and, in the process, discover her own magical abilities.

Past Traumas:

The loss of her parents left her with emotional scars and a sense of abandonment, fueling her need for independence and causing her to resist forming deep bonds. This makes it difficult for her to ask for help or engage in romantic relationships, as shown throughout the novel.

Motivation: What does she want?

Remember: motivation refers to what the character wants. It's their primary goal or what they actively pursue in the plot.

Isabella seeks answers about her parents' death and tries to avoid facing her magical past or having others discover her powers.

Conflict: What does she need?

Remember: conflict arises between what the character needs, often a lesson or internal change, and what they initially seek.

Isabella struggles with the emotional barrier she has built around her heart due to her past traumas. Furthermore, she fears that using her magic may attract unwanted attention from those who wish to exploit or capture her, as they did with her parents. However, she'll be forced to fully master her magical abilities to survive supernatural dangers that lurk and to accept the magical origins she had previously rejected.

Character Arc and Learnings

Remember: throughout the story, the character overcomes trials and traumas and discovers that what they want is not exactly what they need. Thanks to this learning, they will resolve the main problem of the story.

As Isabella embarks on her quest for answers and helps the people she encounters along the way, she learns to overcome her fears and allows others into her life. She discovers that true magic lies in connecting with people and the power to heal through love and trust. She finds love and uncovers the truth about her past.

Appendix:

Images and drawings of Isabella. Isabella communicating with animals, casting magical rays, etc.

PROFILE 2: JAY GATSBY FROM *THE GREAT GATSBY*

(The Great Gatsby by F. Scott Fitzgerald, 1925)

Name: Jay Gatsby

Age: Early thirties

Profession: Millionaire and party host

Physical Description:

Gatsby is a tall, athletic man with a charming smile and eyes that reflect a mixture of mystery and sadness. His clothing and style reflect his wealth and extravagance.

Personality:

Gatsby is enigmatic, charismatic, and obsessed with his past and his love for Daisy Buchanan. Despite his wealth and success, his loneliness and desire to reclaim his past define his character.

Backstory:

Gatsby grew up in poverty and struggled to move up in society. His obsession with Daisy led him to make a fortune and throw extravagant parties to attract her attention.

Past Traumas:

Gatsby is obsessed with the idea of reclaiming the past with Daisy and erasing the barriers that separated them.

Major Flaws:

- Physical: He has an old scar on his right leg, the result of a car accident in his youth.
- Personality: Sometimes, his obsession makes him act impulsively. He lets himself be blinded by his desires and insists upon a course of action when it is clear that it would be better to throw in the towel.

Particular characteristics and unique talents:

Gatsby has an exceptional ability to organize spectacular parties and events that attract everyone's attention. He's very charismatic and always surrounded by an aura of mystery.

Motivation: what does he want?

Remember: motivation refers to what the character wants. It is his primary goal or what he is actively pursuing in the plot.

Gatsby seeks to regain the relationship he had with Daisy years ago. His whole life revolves around winning back her affection.

Conflict:

Remember: conflict arises between what the character needs, often an internal lesson or change, and what he initially seeks.

The conflict arises from Gatsby's desire to regain a past that no longer exists and his inability to accept that Daisy has changed. His denial of reality leads him to inevitable tragedy.

Character arc and learnings

Remember: throughout the story, the character overcomes trials and traumas and discovers that what he wants is not exactly what he needs. Thanks to this learning, he will solve the main problem of the story.

As the story progresses, Gatsby realizes that his dream is unattainable. His obsession consumes him and leads him to tragedy as he discovers the complexities of love and illusion.

Appendix:

Images and drawings of Jay Gatsby.

PROFILE 3: BEATRIZ FROM "HIDDEN NOTES"

Name: Beatriz Expósito.

Age: 58 years old.

Occupation: Unemployed, a businessman's widow. Currently, she's a ghost in search of redemption.

Physical Description:

Beatriz was very beautiful in her youth: slim, with dark eyes and long, black hair; however, after the death of the man she loved, she stopped taking care of herself and turned to alcohol, which gave her a gaunt and neglected appearance.

Personality:

Beatriz is enigmatic, intelligent, and very self-assured. She has a great sense of humor, though always dark and ironic. She's also extremely stubborn and unable to express her feelings.

Background Story:

Beatriz married a man ten years older than her at a very young age, purely driven by physical appearance. However, there was no chemistry between them, and shortly afterward, she fell in love with her husband's business partner.

Past Traumas:

She feels guilty for the death of the man she loved; this guilt led her to alcoholism, which also ruined her daughter's life.

After the tragic end of her secret love affair, she tried to erase all traces of the past and shut herself off from the world to protect her heart.

Main Flaws:

• Physical: A gaunt appearance due to excessive alcohol and the silent guilt carried for years.

• Personality: Stubborn and a poor communicator.

Distinctive Characteristics and Special Abilities:

After her death, Beatriz returns to Earth as a specter, enabling her to appear and disappear, pass through walls, become visible only to certain people, communicate with other deceased, levitate, and more.

Motivation: What does she want?

Beatriz is trapped on Earth until she resolves her unfinished business. Her goal is to tell her daughter the truth about her past actions to be able to move on to the next plane, stop being a ghost, and finally let go of her earthly troubles.

Conflict:

Beatriz's daughter hates her mother for everything she did and is unwilling to help her fulfill her mission. Beatriz will have to offer something in exchange for her cooperation or resign herself to being a ghost forever.

Character Arc and Learnings:

Beatriz realizes that her daughter could learn from her experience because she's on the verge of making mistakes that are very similar to hers. Beatriz understands that what she truly needs is her daughter's forgiveness before leaving Earth. Above all, like all mothers, she needs to know that her daughter loves her despite all the mistakes she has made.

Appendix:

Images and drawings of Beatriz.

Today's task: Step 4

- Study the character sheets from the examples.
- Copy the character sheet you'll find below and complete it. As always, don't feel obligated to fill everything out. Write down what you know or make up anything to have a starting point.

Remember: these sheets are filled out in pencil, and it's normal to revisit them during the process to make changes and improvements.

CHARACTER SHEET

- Name:
  - Does the character have a last name?
  - Is the character known by any other alternative names?
- Age during the novel
- Date of birth
- Background:
- Biography
  - Significant events from their past
- Past traumas
- Motivation: What do they want?
- Conflict: What do they truly need?
- Main flaws:
  - What's preventing them from getting what they want?
  - Unique physical characteristics
  - Distinct personality traits
  - Others
  - How do these flaws/peculiarities limit them?
- Specific characteristics:
  - Magical powers
  - Special talents
- Relationships (past, present, future)
- Character development, lessons:

- o What must they overcome to achieve success?
- o What lesson will they learn at the end of the story?
- Additional notes
- Photographs and drawings.

CHARACTER SHEET

PHOTOS:

NAME:
SURNAME:
ALTERNATIVE NAMES:

DATE OF BIRTH:
PLACE OF BIRTH:
AGE DURING THE NOVEL:

PHYSICAL DESCRIPTION:

PERSONALITY:

SPECIAL TALENTS OR MAGICAL POWERS:

CHARACTER SHEET

BIOGRAPHY

IMPORTANT RELATIONSHIPS, PAST, CURRENT, OR FUTURE:
FAMILY, FRIENDS, PARTNERS…

OTHER RELEVANT DETAILS ABOUT THEIR PAST

CHARACTER SHEET

FLAWS AND AREAS FOR IMPROVEMENT.
(INCLUDE WHY THEY ARE RELEVANT AND HOW THEY LIMIT THEM).

TRAUMAS OR LIMITING BELIEFS

MOTIVATION - WHAT DO THEY WANT?

CONFLICT - WHAT DO THEY NEED?

ⒶCHARACTER SHEET   4/4

CHARACTER DEVELOPMENT.

1) WHAT MUST THEY OVERCOME TO ACHIEVE SUCCESS?

2) WHAT LESSON DO THEY LEARN AT THE END OF THE STORY?

ADDITIONAL NOTES

APPENDIX: PHOTOGRAPHS, DRAWINGS, DIAGRAMS...

CHAPTER FIVE

The ideal breeding ground

"

"Miracles begin to happen when we do the right thing

at the right moment

in the right place."

—Anonymous

The Perfect Setting for Your Story

I would like to begin this chapter with a short story:

"In a futuristic dystopian society, Alice was a dreamy young woman who dreamt of escaping the new and ridiculous laws her government had imposed to control the population. One day, while fleeing constant surveillance, even inside her own home, Alice saw another teenager wearing a rabbit mask. He claimed he was running late for a secret meeting. Driven by curiosity, she followed him and stumbled upon a mysterious technological portal that transported her to an alternate world called 'The Wonderland.' There, she encountered

83

strange cybernetic beings and the immortal hologram of their ruler, the Queen of Hearts, whom she would have to disconnect from the electrical grid in order to end the cruel tyranny that kept all humans as slaves in a fictitious world of virtual reality..."

Sounds familiar?

It's Alice in Wonderland by Lewis Carroll but transported to a dystopian and futuristic setting. Imagine if the author had used the same characters we know from the original book, the same central theme, and even most of the original dialogues but had set the story in a place other than Victorian England. Undoubtedly, the result would have been entirely different from what we know today.

The setting of a story can completely change the flavor, tone, and perception of a tale, even if the plot remains exactly the same. This is evidenced by the fairy tale retelling trend and all the classic books rewritten in a different location or time. For instance, in the novel *These Violent Delights* by Chloe Gong, the author takes the story of Romeo and Juliet and transports it to 1926 Shanghai, where Roma Montagov (Romeo Montague) and Juliette Cai (Juliet Capulet) belong to two rival mafia factions.

In life, as in novels, the right place is as important as the right moment when it comes to achieving success.

Therefore, before you start writing your novel, it's essential to consider the following questions:

- <u>Era</u>: In what era or historical period does the story take place? Undoubtedly, Romeo and Juliet would sound quite different during the Paleolithic period or in the year 2130 in the Triton Galaxy.

- <u>Location</u>: The geographical setting where the events occur. Is it a real or a fantastical place? What is the architecture and the setting like? Think about buildings, natural landscapes, and the constructed environment. If it's a fantasy novel, you'll need to dedicate more time and effort to this aspect.

- <u>Society</u>: Consider the social structure, governments, kings, hierarchies, classes, and roles of the characters in the story.

- <u>Culture</u>: Define the traditions, customs, beliefs, and values of the society portrayed. If it's an imaginary society, you'll need to invent what they are.

- <u>Climate and season</u>: Think about the weather and climatic conditions during the narrative. Are you writing a surfer romance happening during the summer, with your characters swimming near crowded beaches, or during the winter when the coastal town of your protagonists is nearly deserted, and there's nobody else but them walking along those stormy shores?

- <u>Technology</u>: Consider technological advancements or tools used in the world of the story. Do they have cell phones, or do they use carrier pigeons? Do they ride horses, or do they teleport?

- <u>Magic</u>: If supernatural creatures appear in your novel or if any of your characters possess magical powers, it's crucial to have a clear understanding of how these magical powers work: who has them, how they are transmitted, what can and cannot be done, what depletes them, how to defeat a magical creature, etc. Otherwise, inconsistencies can easily arise as the story progresses.

Maps and drawings

On some occasions, it can be constructive to draw plans and maps to help you navigate the city, the country, or even the building where your story unfolds.

- <u>Fantasy Worlds</u>: If your novel takes place in a fantastical country or continent, it will be advantageous to sketch out the locations of the main cities, borders, rivers, mountains, etc. Do it in pencil (I know I keep saying this, but I speak from experience) to allow for changes as the plot evolves. Once you finish your book, send the sketch to a professional illustrator and ask them to create the final map of your world and include it in the book for your readers to refer to.

- <u>Actual Countries and Cities</u>: Even if your story is set in an existing city, it will be beneficial to print out a map of it and mark important locations, for example:

- o The protagonist's house,
- o Their workplace,
- o Places where crimes or disappearances occurred,
- o Restaurants, shops, police stations, and other relevant locations.

How to Differentiate Between Necessary and Superfluous Descriptions

So far, we've discussed the architecture, technology, climate, and many other aspects of your book's location. These aspects, when combined, will help you create a detailed and authentic setting that immerses the reader in the world of your story.

However, remember that all this information is primarily for you, the author. Use it to enrich the story, to make it deeper and more realistic, and to avoid long-term inconsistencies.

But use it with moderation in your descriptions.

Information about the environment, just like the physical details of the characters, should be used like salt in cooking: a pinch enhances the story, but if you overdo it, the dish becomes unpalatable. Nowadays, very few readers have the patience to read pages and pages where the author describes a landscape in every detail. This depends somewhat on the genre—fantasy readers often have a much higher tolerance for descriptions than, for example, thriller readers—but in most cases, the average reader appreciates it if we don't overdo descriptions. At least if you want to maintain suspense and write a book that keeps the reader glued to the pages. The world was very different before the technological revolution when the only alternative to reading a book was watching the rain fall outside the window. Even in our parents' time, people had to resign themselves to watching the only movie shown on TV at the time it was broadcast and endure lengthy interruptions for commercials. It's easy to understand that during that time, slow and descriptive books were much more successful than they are today.

That's why I encourage you to create character and location profiles with as much detail as possible, but I also recommend that you use this content in the form of subtle strokes skillfully scattered throughout the story to avoid boring the reader with endless paragraphs full of adjectives.

Tip:

If you mention some feature of the environment, do it with a purpose in mind, for example:

- <u>Conveying sensations:</u> *"the graveyard was covered by a thick and dark fog..."* (Conveys sadness, terror, or oppression).
- <u>Giving the reader location details they'll need to understand a scene:</u> *"the hallway was narrow, and the exit was blocked..."* (Helps me understand there was no

escape from that hallway and why the character had to turn around and fight the aggressors).

- <u>Developing the novel's theme and symbolic elements:</u> *"The river between the rival towns of Upperville and Lowertown was a turbulent and powerful barrier..."* (The river symbolizes the schism between the two towns).

Every time you're about to describe something, ask yourself if your descriptive paragraph serves any of these purposes.

If not, try to find a way to connect the description to the action or the theme of the story.

Otherwise, I encourage you to consider the possibility of reducing that description to the bare minimum... or (gasp!) erasing it.

Location Sheet

PROFILE 1: VALLARISSIA GELIDA

(Made-up fantasy novel)

Name: Vallarissia Gelida.

Era: Ice Age, in a fantasy world resembling the prehistoric era.

Geographical Location: Vallarissia Gelida is a remote and icy region situated in the northern lands of an imaginary planet called Gelidum. It's composed of vast expanses of frozen tundra, snow-covered mountains, and ice caves. The region's inhabitants live in villages built into the sides of the mountains, seeking protection from the extreme cold. The capital is Vallduria, located in the center of the country.

Society: The society of Vallarissia Gelida is tribal and nomadic, consisting of clans that rely on hunting and fishing for survival. Each clan is led by a chief, and family ties are fundamental. Competition for scarce resources and the struggle against the elements are constant.

Culture: The culture of Vallarissia is deeply rooted in spirituality and nature. The clans worship the spirits of animals and elements, seeking their guidance and protection. Sacred rituals include dances and offerings to ensure successful hunting and fishing.

Climate and Season: Vallarissia Gelida experiences an extremely cold climate year-round, with particularly harsh winters. The region is covered in snow most of the time, creating a white and dazzling landscape.

Technology: Technology in Vallarissia is primitive, based on bone and stone tools. The lack of resources limits the possibilities for technological advancement, and the inhabitants focus on survival in a hostile environment.

Magic: Magic in Vallarissia is related to the spirits of nature. The clan shamans are capable of communicating with these spirits and channeling their energy to heal illnesses and predict future events.

Annex: Images and drawings. Map of the planet Gelidum with the location of Vallarissia. Map of Vallarissia with its different regions and major cities.

PROFILE 2: DISTRICT 12

From the novel *The Hunger Games* by Suzanne Collins (2008), which happens to be one of my favorite books

Name: District 12.

Era: Dystopian future.

Geographical Location: District 12 is one of the twelve districts oppressed by the Capitol in Panem. District 12 is a mining area, impoverished and gloomy, characterized by dilapidated buildings and dusty streets. The population struggles to survive, has barely enough to eat, and daily suffer the oppression of the Capitol.

Society: The society in Panem is divided into social classes, with the residents of District 12 being the most disadvantaged. The Capitol's elite lives in opulence, while the district's inhabitants face food shortages and harsh work in the mines and need to get basic goods in the black market.

Culture: District 12's culture is one of silent resistance. The population keeps their traditions alive and supports each other despite the oppression. *The Hunger Games*, a deadly annual event organized by the Capitol, is a fundamental part of this dystopian culture.

Climate and Season: Seasons vary, but the overall feeling during the novel is of a gray and desolate environment.

Technology: Technology in District 12 is limited compared to the Capitol. The population lacks access to advanced technologies and faces daily challenges to meet their basic needs.

Magic: None.

Annex: Images and drawings. Map of the districts of Panem.

PROFILE 3: LONDON FROM *1984*

From the novel *1984* by George Orwell (1949).

Name: London.

Era: Year 1984, in a dystopian future world imagined by George Orwell 35 years earlier.

Geographical Location: London is the capital of *Airstrip One*, a province of the world superpower known as Oceania. The city is under the totalitarian control of the Party and is a gray and desolate place with deteriorating buildings and constant surveillance.

Society: Society in 1984 London is under the control of the Party, which exercises absolute control over every aspect of people's lives. The population lives in fear and conformity, fearing the omnipresent Big Brother.

Culture: Culture in London has been distorted under the influence of the Party. History is constantly rewritten to fit the Party's narrative, and language is reduced to "Newspeak" to control thought.

Climate and Season: The climate in 1984 London is cold and gray, with a perpetual sense of oppression and darkness.

Technology: Technology in London is dominated by Party surveillance and propaganda. "Telescreens" are present everywhere and transmit Party propaganda, while the population is subject to constant surveillance.

Magic: No magical elements.

Annex: Drawings and images of 1984 London.

95

Today's Tasks: Step 5

Task 1:

Let's reimagine a few existing stories. I invite you to choose a couple of examples and write a story based on them. Use the provided examples or come up with one yourself.

Example 1:

- Original story: *Pride and Prejudice* by Jane Austen, set in 19th-century England.
- New setting: In an exclusive business district in New York in 2022, a young executive on the brink of losing her job falls in love with a wealthy and attractive businessman.

Example 2:

- Original story: *Romeo and Juliet* by William Shakespeare, set in Verona, Italy, in the 16th century.
- New setting: Romeo and Juliet belong to rival families that control the water supply in Brasilia, the global capital in the society of the year 3250.

Example 3:

- Original story: *The Count of Monte Cristo* by Alexandre

Dumas, set in 19th-century France.

- New setting: A futuristic version of *The Count of Monte Cristo* set in a space colony in the year 2123, where an unjustly imprisoned astronaut called Edmund Dantfire escapes from prison, infiltrates the ruling elite, and uses his newfound power to seek revenge.

Example 4:

- Original story: *Hamlet* by William Shakespeare, set in Renaissance Denmark.
- New setting: *Hamlet* set in ancient feudal Japan, where a young samurai must confront corruption and betrayal in his lord's court.

Task 2:

Fill out the following location sheet with the details of your upcoming novel or story.

LOCATION SHEET:

- Place Name
- Era
- Geographic Location
- Society
- Culture
- Climate and Season
- Technology
- Magic
- Annex: Drawings and Maps

# LOCATION SHEET

1/2

NAME

ERA:

GEOGRAPHIC LOCATION:

CLIMATE AND SEASON:

SOCIETY:

LOCATION SHEET

2/2

CULTURE:

TECHNOLOGY:

MAGIC:

ADDITIONAL NOTES:

ANNEX: DRAWINGS AND MAPS

C H A P T E R S I X

The Pillars of Your Novel

"

"You cannot build a great building on a weak foundation."

— Gordon B. Hinckley

In the previous chapters, we analyzed the following key points of your novel:

- **What happened?**
- **To whom?**
- **Where?**

Do you remember the four basic pillars we discussed in Chapter 3? If not, don't worry: I added the same image again on the following page for those in the class who already forgot.

Now, we're going to bring together everything we have learned in the previous chapters and build on it.

In this chapter, we will create a basic plot in a table format based on the first three key questions: who, where, and what.

At first sight, this might seem a very basic and unnecessary step, but don't be fooled by the apparent simplicity of the exercise. This IS an important step, and I recommend you don't skip it, as it will help you create a clear and comprehensive overview of your whole story and make your work much easier later on.

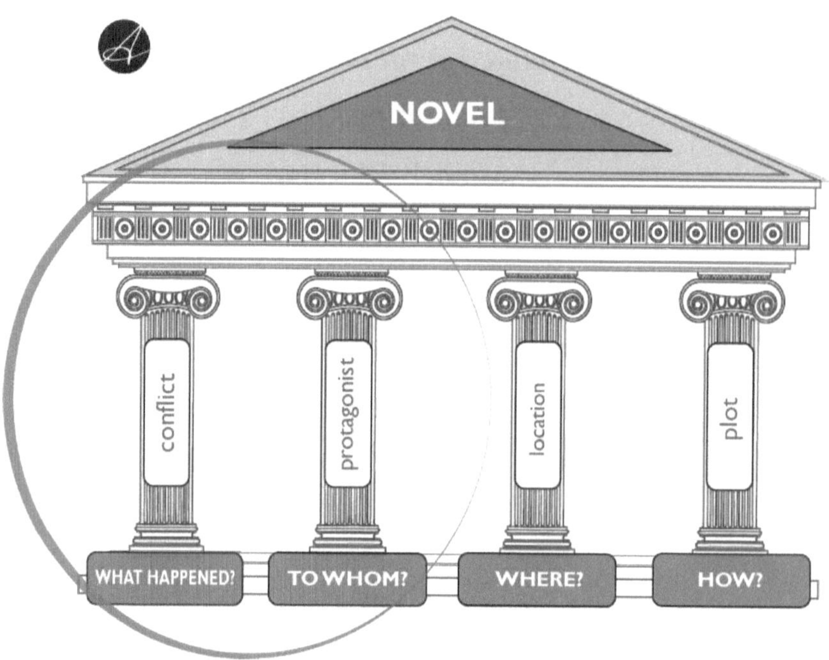

The *WhoWhereCon* Worksheet

I admit it: I could have thought of a better name for this worksheet had I taken the time to do so. But the silly name has an advantage: you'll remember it easily. This worksheet is much more helpful than it seems at first sight, and you'll soon find out why. You might have filled in similar tables at school (I bet you know the five W's from English class[1], so we won't do that one here). Trust me: we're going to go the extra mile and do something a bit different than you did there—and hopefully better—in this chapter.

This chapter was born from a revealing conversation with a fellow author. She was struggling to write a description of her novel for an online newspaper article.

Later, I found out she wasn't an exception: like her, many authors, even the experienced ones, find it challenging to summarize their stories in a few words.

For the uninitiated, it's a bit amusing to think that someone can write four hundred pages of made-up adventures and then get stuck when asked, ***"So, what's your book about?"***

However, this happens quite often, and, as Horatio would say, when this happens, it's a sign that *something is rotten in the state of Denmark.*

---

[1] Who, What, When Where, and Why

But I have good news for you: once you complete this chapter and the next one, you'll never find yourself in this situation again.

WHOWHERECON FLICT

WhoWhereCon is an abbreviation of the main elements in this table:

- WHO: here, we describe the protagonist.
- WHERE: here, we describe the setting.
- CONFLICT: here, we describe what happens in the story (the main issue that needs to be solved).

We're going to use this form to summarize a story in the basic points of who, where, and conflict.

You can also use it to:

- Analyze existing stories.
- Gain clarity during the planning phase.
- Write an efficient description of your already written novel.

In this chapter, we'll see examples of the first two uses. The third use will be addressed in a separate chapter dedicated to writing a good synopsis.

Let's now see the WhoWhereCon worksheet in action. Read the examples carefully, and once you finish, try to come up with new ones on your own.

Example 1: Cinderella

Folk Tale

WHO:

Cinderella, a beautiful young girl who lives in poverty, mistreated by her stepmother and stepsisters since her mother's death.

WHERE:

An imaginary feudal kingdom in the Middle Ages.

PROBLEM TO SOLVE:

Cinderella's only chance to escape her miserable life is to attend the royal ball and capture the prince's attention. Her fairy godmother provides her with a magical dress and carriage to help her in her mission. However, she only has until midnight to make the prince fall in love with her before the enchantment on her dress vanishes.

Example 2: Moby Dick

A novel by Herman Melville

WHO:

Captain Ahab, a middle-aged American sailor who lost a leg and is obsessed with hunting the great white whale, Moby Dick.

WHERE:

A whaling ship that sails the Pacific and Atlantic oceans in the mid-19th century.

PROBLEM TO SOLVE:

Captain Ahab is consumed by his obsession with seeking revenge on Moby Dick, the whale that took his leg.

Example 3: Pride and Prejudice

Novel by Jane Austen

WHO: Since it's a romantic novel, it's helpful to know the characteristics and motivations of both members of the couple.

1. Elizabeth Bennet, an intelligent and free-spirited woman who must marry as soon as possible to meet the social expectations of her time. However, Elizabeth refuses to settle for a marriage of convenience.

2. Mr. Darcy, a reserved and arrogant nobleman who believes that women are only interested in his money. Deep down, he has a tender heart, but he hides his sensitivity to protect himself from pain.

WHERE:

The English countryside and the circles in which the well-to-do English society of the 19th century used to mingle.

> PROBLEM TO SOLVE:
>
> - Elizabeth must overcome her prejudices towards Darcy.
> - Mr. Darcy must swallow his pride and show his sensitive side to Elizabeth.
> - Only then can they find true love!

Today's task: Step 6

- Choose two stories for this exercise:
  - A book you have read.
  - A novel you are currently planning or writing.
- Answer the following questions in your notebook. There's a blank table ready on the next page.
  - WHO: who is the protagonist of the story?
  - WHERE: where and when do the events take place?
  - CONFLICT: what is the biggest problem your protagonist has to solve?

TITLE:

WHO:

WHERE:

PROBLEM TO SOLVE:

C H A P T E R S E V E N

Writing a great synopsis

"

"Simplicity is the ultimate sophistication."
—Leonardo da Vinci

Have you ever heard of the expression "**elevator pitch**"? With this term, we refer to a brief phrase capable of describing an idea or project (usually a business idea or a commercial product) in a concise and appealing manner.

The name "elevator pitch" comes from the fact that this phrase should be:

- **Short enough** to recite to a stranger in an elevator during the time it takes to ride a couple of floors.
- Additionally, it should be **attractive enough** for said stranger to become your customer or investor, or at least to pique their interest in that very brief time.

As a writer, you will often be asked to explain what your novel is about. You'll need to have this response prepared when offering your book to potential publishers, film producers, and, of course, readers. If you self-publish, you'll also need to describe your novel on social media and on the book's back cover. Furthermore, having a compelling and memorable synopsis will be crucial when writing the dreaded *blurb*, which is the description of your book that will appear on the websites where it's sold and in many other places. **A persuasive and memorable synopsis will be key to making a potential reader choose your novel or pass it** by and forget about it forever.

Not only that, but a clear description will also be beneficial during the writing process, as it will help you define your goal and stay on track without deviating from the main idea.

In this chapter, I'll help you create a brief and concise description of your story. You might think it's a bit early to take this step, but trust me, the perfect time is **now**.

The diagram below shows each step of the method we'll follow:

In the previous chapters, we answered the first three questions:

- What happened? (Conflict)
- To whom? (Main characters)
- Where? (Location)

Then, we created the *WhoWhereCon* worksheets.

Now, we can move on to the next step: composing a synopsis of the story.

This synopsis will evolve as you refine the draft, and the final version may be very different from the initial one. However, the procedure for creating it is always the same, and we'll start with the WhoWhereCon worksheet we filled out earlier.

The Subtle Art of Summarizing Your Book in One Sentence

A good synopsis should include information about **who** is involved, **where** the events occur, and **what problem** needs to be solved.

The basic outline to create such sentences is as follows:

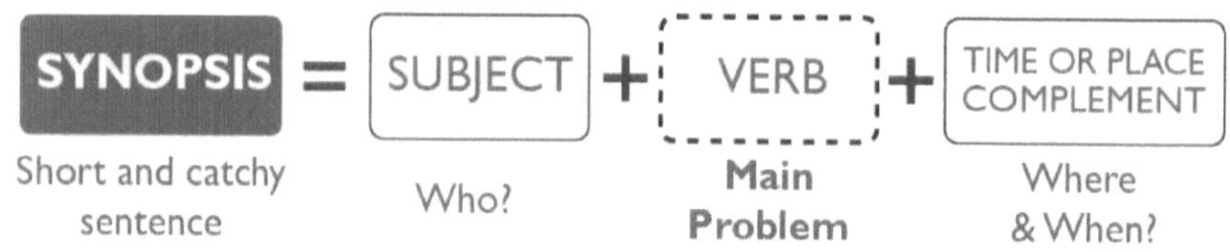

In other words:

- SUBJECT (who)
- VERB (problem)
- TIME OR PLACE COMPLEMENT (where and when)

The verb is particularly important: choose it carefully so that it introduces conflict, mystery, or emotion. A well-chosen verb will quickly capture the reader's attention. For example, in the following synopsis, we say that the protagonist is *struggling to survive*, which immediately creates interest and curiosity:

<u>The Handmaid's Tale by Margaret Atwood</u>

"In a dystopian future (when), a woman named Offred (who) <u>struggles to survive</u> (what) in a totalitarian society where women are subjugated and used as reproductive instruments (where)."

Tricks for Writing an Intriguing Synopsis

I recommend using at least one of the following tools when writing your synopsis, as it will automatically make it more effective and engaging:

- **Countdown**: Make it clear that the character has limited time to achieve their goal. For example, Cinderella has <u>only until midnight</u> to win the prince's heart.
- **Emotional Connection**: Describe the intensity of the character's feelings (positive or negative) toward something or someone. For example, Captain Ahab feels <u>hatred and a desire for revenge</u>.
- **Aura of Mystery**: Leave the reader wanting to know more. In *Murder on the Orient Express*, we want to <u>find out who the murderer is and why</u> they did it.

Decide which of these three *tricks* best suits your story, and use at least one when writing the description. Once you have the first draft, move on to the next section and check that your summary contains **the 6 essential characteristics of a good synopsis.**

6 Essential Characteristics of a Good Synopsis

<u>A good synopsis should meet all the points on this list.</u> Once you have written yours, return to this section and make sure it includes these six key traits:

1. **Conciseness**: A synopsis should be brief and direct. Depending on its purpose, you can extend it to a paragraph or two, but for our planning exercise, we'll

strive to summarize the book's concept <u>in one or two sentences at most</u>. Every word counts, so edit and revise your synopsis to make it as clear and concise as possible. Remove all superfluous words until it's perfect.

2. **Conflict**: Describe the main obstacle the protagonist must face.

3. **Character**: Introduce the protagonist and their motivations.

4. **Twist or Hook:** Highlight unexpected twists or mysterious occurrences to capture the reader's attention.

5. **Avoid Revealing Too Much (No Spoilers)**: It's often said that *clothing that suggests the figure but leaves something to the imagination is more attractive and sexier than clothing that reveals everything*. The same applies to a book's description: reveal only a little and let the readers ask themselves questions to generate more interest. Leave something for their imagination. Make them wonder.

6. **Style and Voice**: If possible, reflect the tone and style of your novel. For example, in a humorous novel, try to write a funny synopsis; in a mystery novel, create suspense, and so on.

Now, I invite you to go back to the previous chapter and review the WhoWhereCon tables (remember: who, where, and conflict).

These worksheets make creating a synopsis very easy since we already have the story broken down and ready to create a sentence. Like this:

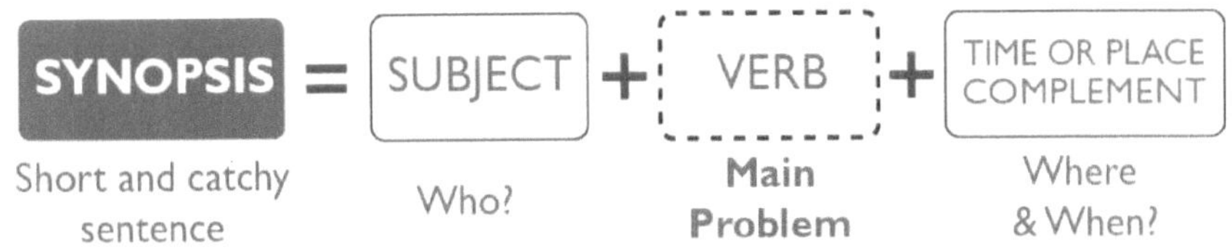

Let's see how to put it into practice (using the examples from the worksheets at the end of the previous chapter):

Cinderella

Cinderella, a young woman mistreated by her stepmother and stepsisters, receives magical help from her fairy godmother to attend a royal ball, win the prince's heart, and escape poverty. However, she must achieve her goal before the spell vanishes at midnight.

Moby Dick

Captain Ahab, a seafarer who commands a whaling ship, is obsessed with capturing the great white whale Moby Dick to seek revenge for the day it took his leg.

Pride and Prejudice

Elizabeth Bennet, an intelligent and spirited woman from the 19th century, must overcome her prejudices toward Mr. Darcy, a reserved and arrogant yet sensitive nobleman. In turn, Darcy must swallow his pride and reveal his tender side to Elizabeth so they can find true love together.

Task for today: Step 7

- Using the WhoWhereCon worksheet, you filled out in the previous chapter, try to create a sentence that describes your story using the following structure:

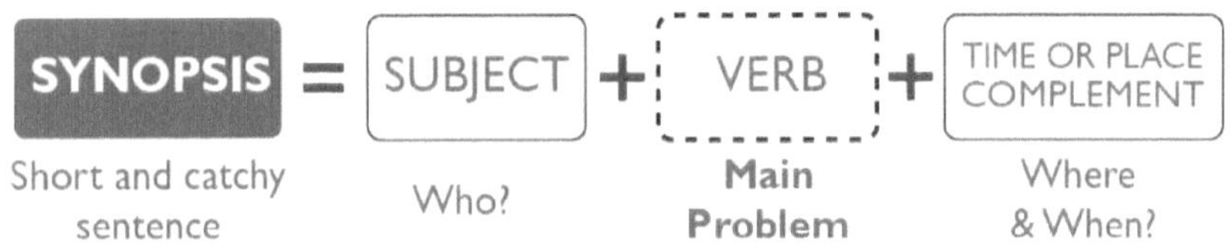

- Make sure you've used an element that creates interest, excitement, or suspense, for example:
    - Countdown
    - Appealing to the reader's emotions
    - Creating mystery and unanswered questions

Repeat the process with other examples: the more, the better. You can use stories you've already written or read, make up your own stories, or use movies you've seen.

CHECKLIST "THE PERFECT SYNOPSIS"

TITLE:

SYNOPSIS:

CHECKLIST:

1	Concise	✓
2	Describes the main conflict	
3	Introduces the protagonist	
4	Includes a twist, hook, or mystery that captures attention	
5	Does not reveal too much (no spoilers)	
6	Style and tone in line with the novel	

© Eva Alton 2023

AUTORISSIMO

C H A P T E R   E I G H T

Plotting the Perfect Plot

"

***"There is a dreadful period of about three weeks or a
month which you have to go through when you start a
book. It is a most extraordinary agony. You are in a state
of unsatisfied restlessness; you are moody and grumpy;
you seem to be waiting for something that never happens,
and you are up in the night, and down in the day, and in
the middle of the night, and in the middle of the day... You
sit in a room, biting pencils and looking at a typewriter, or
you throw yourself on a sofa, with your face to the wall,
and feel like howling until you are sick..."***

— Agatha Christie: An Autobiography

When I started fantasizing about this book several years ago, I
was indeed in one of those moments that the great Agatha talks
about in her autobiography: those moments when writers bite
pencils, throw keyboards out the window, and collapse on the
sofa, ready to tear their manuscript to shreds and start a new
story because they don't know how to continue the current one.

It was then that I began writing in my ***magic notebook***, where I simplified the creative process to the maximum and drew dozens of tables and diagrams to use for my future stories. All of this later gave rise to the method I'm presenting in this book. Since then, every time I sit down to write, I have that same notebook with me—it's not particularly pretty, but it gets the job done efficiently. A few months ago, I thought of condensing that notebook into a practical manual that other people could use, too. My goal was to help other writers minimize those moments of biting pencils and throwing keyboards out the window—good keyboards aren't cheap, after all.

In the previous chapters, we laid the central foundations of a story, exploring the characters, the setting, and the key conflict needed to build a good plot.

With these steps, we clarified the following main questions:

- **What is the predominant genre of my story?**
- **What is the central conflict?**
- **Who are the protagonists?**
- **Where does the story take place?**
- **How can I summarize my story in a few words?**

It's not a coincidence that I left the most important question for last. ***This question is: How did everything happen?***

To answer it, we'll need to delve into the very heart of the story and unravel all its intricacies, complications, and connections.

The most eagerly anticipated and feared moment of this book has arrived...

[Please play the "jump scare" sound here.]

...It's time to plan the plot in detail!

But how?

There are various approaches to developing a plot, and each writer tends to prefer one over the other. In my case, I have experimented in the past with multiple systems, such as the *Hero's Journey*, three and four-act structures, snowflake-like plots that expand exponentially, the uber-famous *Save the Cat!* screenwriting method, and a few more. They all have their advantages and disadvantages, and I used to get stuck at some point with all of them. That's why I'm proposing a similar but slightly different method: it's the one I use, and it has the advantage of being very easy to apply. I call it the Authorissimo method, and I use the *CHRYSALIS* plot.

Why *CHRYSALIS*? Keep reading, and I'll explain everything.

Common Narrative Structures

This is probably not the first book you've read on writing, and you've likely heard of the most common structures used for creating a plot. Nevertheless, it won't hurt to review them briefly before we continue. As you may already know, some of the most commonly used plot structures include:

The Three or Four-Act Structure

This is one of the oldest structures and has been used for centuries throughout history. It generally works like this:

- Act 1 - Setup: This is where we introduce the protagonist, the conflict, and the world in which the story will take place.

- Act 2 - Confrontation: Complications and conflicts arise, leading the protagonist to the lowest point of their journey.

- Act 3 - Climax and Resolution: The protagonist confronts the main antagonist and resolves the conflict.

Some authors prefer to use a four-act structure, which is very similar but includes an additional middle act (Act 3 being the climax and Act 4 the resolution of the conflict).

The Hero's Journey

The plotted story revolves around a hero (the protagonist) who embarks on a journey, faces challenges, and returns home transformed. It's an ancient archetype found in myths and legends from around the world and has existed for centuries, although it was Joseph Campbell who popularized it. In his book *The Hero with a Thousand Faces* (1949), he identified recurring patterns in myths and legends from different cultures and described *The Hero's Journey* as we know it today. Of course, the protagonist doesn't necessarily have to be *a hero* in the literal sense of the word, and their journey can be metaphorical—they don't need to leave their home in the literal sense. The plot is structured as follows:

- Call to Adventure: The protagonist receives a call to embark on a journey (real or metaphorical).

- Refusal of the Call: The protagonist often doubts or refuses to answer the call.

- Crossing the Threshold: The protagonist eventually decides to embark on the adventure.

- Tests, Allies, and Enemies: In the middle part of the story, conflicts and learning experiences occur. The protagonist encounters allies and enemies and fights small battles.

- Climax and Resolution: The decisive moment arrives, leading to the transformation of the protagonist, enabling them to emerge victorious.

- The Return: The protagonist returns home with a new perspective and skills, transformed into a hero (not necessarily a literal hero).

The Save the Cat Method

The "Save the Cat" system was created by Blake Snyder, a screenwriter and author, and he describes it in his book *Save the Cat!* (2005). Initially, he developed it for creating movie scripts, but many writers adopted it for planning their novels. A unique and original characteristic of this method is to have the protagonist "save a cat" at the beginning of the movie or novel. To do this, he presents the protagonist as a flawed human who makes mistakes but ensures they perform a selfless act at the beginning of the story (for example, but not limited to rescuing a kitten stuck in a tree). This automatically generates empathy from the viewer or reader, who will side with the character because they have seen their good-hearted nature. This emotional connection makes the reader interested in the protagonist's success at the end of the story and supports them throughout their journey.

The Snowflake Method

This method, less known but highly original, was developed by Randy Ingermanson, a novelist and non-fiction writer. He describes the technique in his book *How to Write a Novel Using the Snowflake Method* (2014). This is a unique method, different from the previous ones, where the author starts with a simple concept and expands on it. For example, you can begin by describing your story in one sentence, then expand it to an entire page, then to five pages, and so on, until it becomes extensive enough to serve as the first draft of your story.

If you haven't read them already, I recommend getting all the books mentioned in this section because they will be very useful in your writing career.

In the next section, I'll show you my method for planning a plot and teach you how to work with the worksheets from this book.

The *Chrysalis* Plot

I'm going to present you with a straightforward and effective system for planning the chapters and scenes of your story. **It's a holistic approach focused on the character's transformation throughout the story, and the plot we'll create will be born from the combination of motivation and conflict.**

In this method, the *protagonist's metamorphosis* becomes the driving force of the novel, and no event occurs without reason or cause.

I like to think of characters at the beginning of a story as small caterpillars wandering through their ordinary world, unaware of what awaits them. They mistakenly believe they are just ordinary worms, but in reality, they carry the potential to become much more. Over the course of a good novel, the protagonist must undergo a profound transformation as a result of the adventures they experience. This is why I named this structure *the Chrysalis Plot.*

Chrysalis Plot:

"An evolving plot in which characters transition from being mere caterpillars to transforming into extraordinary butterflies, traversing the frightening darkness of the chrysalis until they are capable of emerging from it on their own and take flight with their newly discovered wings."

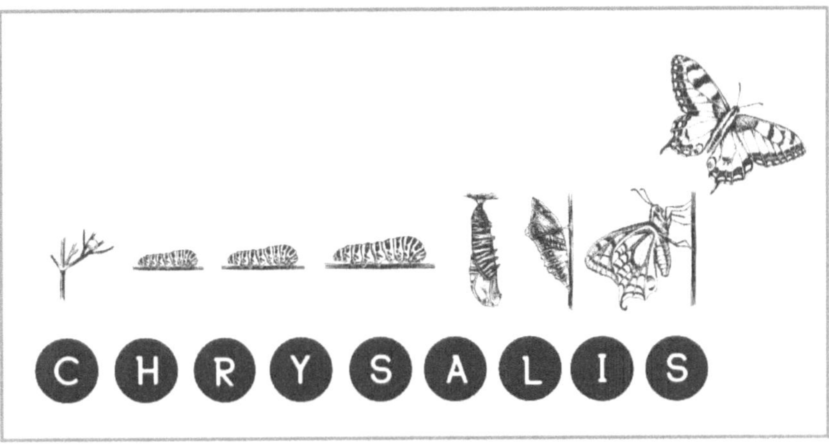

You will find it very easy to remember the name and order of the segments in which we will divide the plot because they form an acronym for the word CHRYSALIS, as we'll see below.

We're going to divide the plot into nine segments that will guide the narrative flow of the story. Each one symbolizes a step forward in the transformation of the protagonist. This personal transformation is the vortex around which the entire plot will revolve, and it will help you write more profound stories that create empathy in the reader for the protagonist during their journey. The goal is to write more compelling stories that maintain suspense throughout the narrative. Moreover, by using this method, you'll find that the planning and creation process becomes much faster.

Narrative Metamorphosis Segments

When I talk about *Narrative Metamorphosis*, I'm referring to the process of change and growth that the protagonist undergoes throughout the story. In most well-known stories, we can identify nine key segments, and I've used their initials to create the word CHRYSALIS. My goal is only to make it easier for you to remember them. They are:

- <u>C - Commencement and Introduction</u>
- <u>H - Herald of Change</u>
- <u>R - Road to Transformation</u>
- <u>Y - Yearning for Adventure</u>
- <u>S - Shift of Perspective</u>
- <u>A - Aggravation of the Conflict</u>
- <u>L - Lowest Point of the Journey</u>
- <u>I - Illuminating Revelation</u>
- <u>S - Soaring in Triumph</u>

CHARACTER METAMORPHOSIS
COMMENCEMENT
C
Motivation: "I want..."
0%
HERALD OF CHANGE
H
MY LIFE IS NOT ENOUGH
I DREAM OF BETTER THINGS
ROAD TO TRANSFORMATION
R
"This is all new and exciting!"
25%
YEARNING FOR ADVENTURE
Y
TRIALS
MENTORS
LESSONS
SMALL VICTORIES
SMALL DEFEATS
SHIFT OF PERSPECTIVE
S
"My motivation is faltering..."
50%
AGGRAVATION OF THE CONFLICT
A
MORE TRIALS
THIS IS HARDER THAN I EXPECTED
I DON'T KNOW WHAT TO DO ANYMORE
SHOULD I GIVE UP?
"I'm desperate."
INTROSPECCION AND DARKEST HOUR
L
"Wait a minute..."
75%
LOWEST POINT
I
"I've learned my lesson at last."
SOARING IN TRIUMPH
S
100%
LEARNING GROWING METAMORPHOSIS
© Eva Alton 2023

The 9 segments of the Chrysalis *plot*

- **C - Commencement and Introduction**: At the beginning of the narrative, we introduce the protagonist and their surroundings. Right now, they're much like a caterpillar moving through its familiar environment. And just like caterpillars do, they lead a mundane life. But there's something that hints they're not an ordinary worm and have the potential to transform into something better. Through this phase, we suggest the central themes that will resonate throughout their metamorphosis during the story.

- **H - Herald of Change**: In this stage, a disruption shatters the protagonist's routine, propelling them to make a brave decision and venture into the unknown, much like a caterpillar abandoning its habitual path. This is where ***the protagonist figures out they want something.***

- **R - Road to Transformation**: Here, the protagonist embarks on a new odyssey, immersing themselves in an unfamiliar world where they'll have to acquire skills and form alliances.

- **Y - Yearning for Adventure**: In this phase, the protagonist enters an uncharted territory filled with challenges and opportunities. While gaining new abilities and forging crucial connections, their journey mirrors that of **a caterpillar on a path to metamorphosis**. Things become interesting, and the main character jumps in with both feet.

- **S - Shift of Perspective:** As the story progresses, a significant alteration or shift takes place, amplifying the tension and complicating the protagonist's path. Suddenly, things aren't as fun as they were at the beginning. **Things are not what they seemed at first.**

- **A - Aggravation of the Conflict**: The conflict intensifies, presenting the protagonist with more challenging and complex trials, pushing the narrative to higher levels of emotions and difficulties. **This isn't going to be as easy as the protagonist thought, and a change is needed.**

- **L - Lowest Point of the Journey**: We reach the nadir of the protagonist's journey, usually occurring at around 75% of the story. Here, they are forced to confront their internal weaknesses and fears, driving them toward a significant internal change. **Similar to how the**

caterpillar goes through the darkness of the chrysalis during its transformation, this stage challenges the protagonist to face their own darkness to emerge transformed.

- **I - Illuminating Revelation**: This stage (the light bulb moment) marks the culmination of the narrative, where the protagonist reaches a crucial revelation. *They discover what they truly need,* motivating them to confront the antagonist or overcome the final obstacle with the skills and wisdom acquired during the previous phases.

- **S - Soaring in Triumph**: After the final confrontation, the protagonist faces the consequences of their choices and experiences emotional closure. This is also a moment of reflection, ideal for connecting with the story's central theme and demonstrating how the character has evolved throughout their journey. **Just as a butterfly takes flight in its new life**, the protagonist finds themselves in a new world, the result of their adventures and learning experiences.

Explanation of each segment and its key points

- **(C) Commencement and Introduction (10% of the novel):** *a presentation of the protagonist and their world.*
    - We introduce the protagonist living their ordinary life before the adventure begins. We show that they are not entirely happy and have flaws but also carry within them the seed that could make them someone special.
    - This is where we first hint at the main theme of the novel.
    - ***The Starting Gun***: It's essential to create intrigue or interest in the story or the protagonist during the first pages of the book and avoid boring or purely descriptive initial chapters. Use this segment to pose key questions or introduce a mystery.
- **(H) Herald of Change (15% of the novel):** *this segment signifies a disturbance of the established order and the decision to embark on a journey (figured or literal).*
    - Disruption of the established order: a disruptive event occurs that prevents the protagonist from continuing their life as it was and forces them to make a change. *The herald of change* can be good or bad, but for

the character, it's an event that <u>disrupts the balance of their routine life,</u> such as meeting a very attractive stranger, discovering they have supernatural powers, receiving an intriguing job offer, losing their job, having a traffic accident, being diagnosed with an illness, receiving unexpected news, learning a secret, etc. Whatever it is, it's going to bring a **change** in their lives.

  o ***We discover what the character WANTS:*** their initial want is related to the disturbance: they want to overcome their illness, rob a bank, rescue their kidnapped wife, etc.

- **(R) Road to Transformation:** *the protagonist makes a brave decision and decides to embark on a journey that is bound to change them forever.*

  o This is where our main character decides to start an adventure or do something they've never done before. ***They do it because they want to achieve what they WANT.***

  o Generally, it's not a hasty decision but involves a process.

  o Often, the character initially refuses to venture but eventually accepts the challenge.

  o Typically, this decision results from the same event that disrupted the order, such as accepting the dangerous job offered or embarking on a trip around the world when they find out they have only four weeks left to live.

- **(Y) Yearning for Adventure:** *Here is where the fun truly begins!*
  - This segment, together with the next three (Y, S, A, L), make up approximately 50% of the story and form its central body.
  - In segment Y, "Yearning for Adventure," the protagonist has embarked on their new adventure and must face trial after trial. These challenges will differ depending on the genre (if it's a war novel, we'll read about battles; if it's a Regency romance, there will be dances, conversations, secret encounters, etc.).
  - *The first trials and setbacks appear, but the character tends to take them lightly—they have no idea what really awaits them on the way.*
  - The character has just begun their journey and is in a different world or situation from their ordinary life. During this part, they must learn to navigate their new life, seek people to help them, gain skills to overcome the enemy, start investigating a murder, plan a wedding with their best friend's ex-boyfriend, etc.

- The character's new world can be real or figurative: they can land on another planet or embark on an actual journey to another country, but they can also stay in their home, sitting on the same couch as at the beginning, now transformed into a member of a resistance group hacking the government's computers in a dystopian world.

- **(S) Shift of Perspective / Significant Upheaval (usually occurs around the midpoint of the novel, around 50%): We find ourselves at the story's central point.**
  - This is where a key event usually occurs that creates a **significant plot twist.**
    - *In a romantic novel*, this is where the characters finally kiss or sleep together after half a book of emotional tension.
    - *In a detective novel*, this is where the investigators find a surprising clue that unexpectedly changes the investigation.
    - *In a thriller*, the protagonist might discover that their best friend has been betraying them.
  - The important thing is that **once this twist occurs, the level of tension or danger must increase.**
  - **This event marks the beginning of the second half of the novel**, where things are going to get

even more challenging for the character.

- **(A) Aggravation of the Conflict / Aggravation of the Struggle: Here, the situation worsens, and the trials become increasingly difficult for the protagonist.**
  - o The path is filled with more and more obstacles, and **the search becomes more urgent**.
    - ▪ Time is running out.
    - ▪ Allies betray them.
    - ▪ Crucial clues lead to dead ends.
    - ▪ Injuries are so severe that they prevent further progress.
  - o **They begin to consider giving up.** And this is how we reach...
- **(L) Lowest Point of the Journey, the moment of deep introspection, the character's darkest hour.**
  - o The "Darkest Hour," or the moment of total desperation, **usually occurs when we're about 75% through the story**.
  - o *The Darkest Hour*: At this point, the protagonist typically reaches their lowest point. Things have been deteriorating during the second half, and now it seems they will never achieve their goal. They have lost everything, and no hope is in sight.
    - ▪ If it's a romantic novel, the relationship seems irreparable;
    - ▪ If it's an adventure novel, by this point, we think the protagonist has no escape or is

going to die, etc.

- o Toward the end of this segment, **the character is forced to go into deep introspection** to pull themselves out of the hole they've fallen into.

- **(I) Illuminating Revelation (the light bulb moment, the moment where the lesson is finally understood). This segment and the following make up the final 25% of the text:**
  - o *The Revelation: the character finally realizes what they NEED.* With all the information they've gathered during the central part of the novel, they reach a revealing conclusion.
    - They discover their inner strength, the truth about their dilemma, or a hidden power;
    - They understand that they don't want to get back together with their ex-lover, and what they really need to do is reciprocate the love of that friend they had ignored until now;
    - They complete the puzzle of the clues left by the killer and discover who the culprit is and who will be the next victim, etc.
  - o *The Final Confrontation*: we're in the home stretch of the novel. This part should be **a frantic race against time or the elements** in which the protagonist tries to resolve the situation. This is where they pursue the killer, build a

superpowerful weapon to defeat the villain who wants to dominate the world, or steal a car to sabotage the wedding of the woman they love, about to marry for money after being ignored by them for years.

- o **It's important that this part is not easy**. <u>The protagonist has learned the lesson (had their revelation), but now it's when all the skills they learned during the adventures of the first half and all the clues they gathered at the beginning of the journey come into play.</u>

- **(S) Soaring in Triumph:** *This segment includes the final image with which the adventure ends.*
  - o We offer the reader a view of the protagonist at the end of their journey.
  - o It can be a happy ending or not, depending on the genre; that's not important—the thing that matters the most is that the protagonist must have learned something after going through all those lessons and extreme situations.
  - o Once here, it's essential to return to the central theme of the novel, providing answers to the philosophical questions hinted at in the beginning.

Examples of the CHRYSALIS plot in use

This plot structure is adaptable to almost any story you can think of. Let's have a look at some examples.

"Snow White"

C - Commencement and Introduction: The story begins with Snow White living with her stepmother, the Evil Queen, who is obsessed with being the fairest in the land.

H - Herald of Change: The Evil Queen learns that Snow White is more beautiful than her and decides to kill her to remain *the fairest of them all.*

R - Road to Transformation: Snow White flees into the forest, where she encounters the seven dwarfs.

Y - Yearning for Adventure: Snow White lives with the dwarfs, learns new skills, and starts to adapt and find happiness in her new life.

S - Shift of Perspective: The Evil Queen discovers that Snow White is still alive and plots a way to get rid of the princess herself.

A - Aggravation of the Conflict: The Evil Queen disguises herself as a witch and offers Snow White a poisoned apple. Snow White eats the apple and falls into a deep sleep.

L - Lowest Point of the Journey: Snow White seems dead in her sleep. There appears to be no salvation for her. Her sad story reaches people in distant places, including a brave prince.

I – Illuminating Revelation: The prince arrives, falls in love with Snow White, and kisses her. His true love's kiss saves Snow White. The revelation is that love is stronger than hate or envy.

S - Soaring in Triumph: Snow White finds harmony by marrying the prince and living happily ever after. Love prevails. The Evil Queen, a representation of hatred and envy, is defeated.

"Little Women" by Louisa May Alcott

C - Commencement and Introduction: The story introduces the four March sisters and their daily life during the American Civil War.

H - Herald of Change: The girls' father goes to war, which drastically changes their family's life for the worse.

R – Road to Transformation: The March sisters need to change their habits in order to keep their home and take care of each other in these challenging times.

Y – Yearning for Adventure: The girls experience new challenges but also opportunities as they grow and face life; they also meet boys and learn new skills.

S – Shift of Perspective: The eldest sister, Meg, gets married and leaves home, marking a turning point in their lives.

A – Aggravation of the Conflict: One of the sisters, Beth, becomes seriously ill, and they start to face terrible financial difficulties.

L – Lowest Point of the Journey: Beth, the third of the four sisters, dies, and it seems like they will never be happy again or fulfill their dreams.

I – Illuminating Revelation: Each sister grapples with their own aspirations and personal limitations, seeking a way out. Jo, the protagonist, focuses on her career as a writer after her sister's death.

S - Soaring in Triumph: Jo and her sisters reconcile with the loss of Beth and find happiness, each sister in her own way.

"The Da Vinci Code" by Dan Brown

C - Commencement and Introduction: The story introduces Professor Robert Langdon in his everyday life, signing books and teaching about ancient symbology.

H - Herald of Change: A man is murdered in the Louvre, and he writes Langdon's name in his own blood before dying, making Langdon a suspect in the murder.

R – Road to Transformation: French Inspector Sophie Neveu urges Professor Langdon to flee from the police and investigate on his own to avoid being blamed for a crime he didn't commit.

Y – Yearning for Adventure: Langdon and Sophie uncover secrets and conspiracies as the investigation progresses. They become increasingly interested in the mystery at hand.

S – Shift of Perspective: The truth about the lineage of Jesus and his relationship with Mary Magdalene shakes their understanding of Christianity and their theories about the murder at the Louvre.

A – Aggravation of the Conflict: Langdon and Sophie realize they are being pursued by a secret organization and must fight for their lives while still seeking answers.

L – Lowest Point of the Journey: Langdon and Sophie reach a point where there seems to be no way out, cornered between the police accusing them of murder and their former ally, who has also turned against them in order to seize the Holy Grail.

I – Illuminating Revelation: Langdon has a revelation. He discovers the truth about the Holy Grail and where it is located.

S - Soaring in Triumph: Langdon and Sophie find harmony by revealing the truth and solving the mystery. Sophie finds her family. Langdon's career and beliefs are changed forever.

Today's Task: Step 8

Your turn!

Use your own story, a book you have read, or a movie you watched recently and complete the nine plot segments:

- C - Commencement and Introduction
- H - Herald of Change
- R - Road to Transformation
- Y - Yearning for Adventure
- S - Shift of Perspective
- A - Aggravation of the Conflict
- L - Lowest Point of the Journey
- I - Illuminating Revelation
- S - Soaring in Triumph

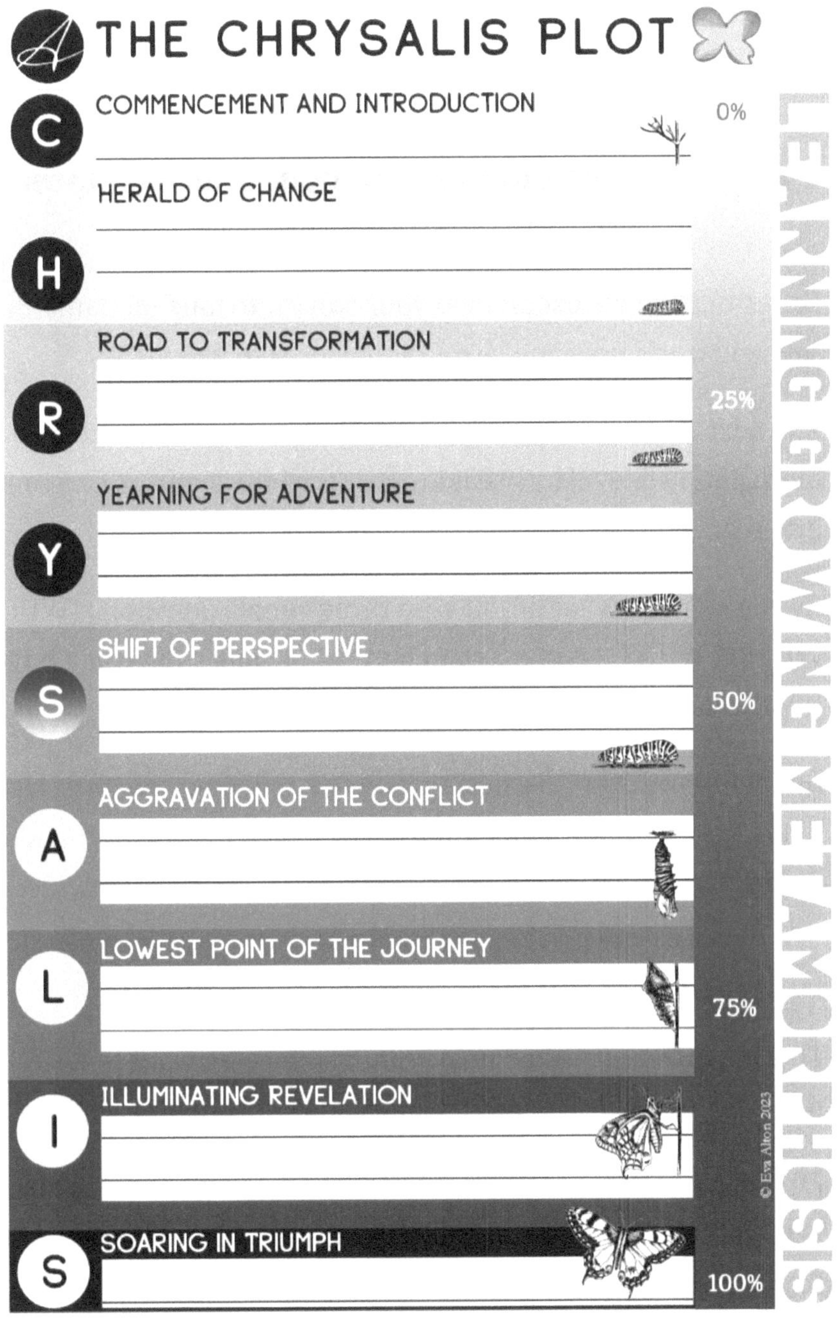
THE CHRYSALIS PLOT
COMMENCEMENT AND INTRODUCTION
0%
C
HERALD OF CHANGE
H
ROAD TO TRANSFORMATION
25%
R
YEARNING FOR ADVENTURE
Y
SHIFT OF PERSPECTIVE
50%
S
AGGRAVATION OF THE CONFLICT
A
LOWEST POINT OF THE JOURNEY
75%
L
ILLUMINATING REVELATION
I
SOARING IN TRIUMPH
S
100%
LEARNING GROWING METAMORPHOSIS
© Eva Alton 2023

CHAPTER NINE

Chapters and Scenes

Developing the Chrysalis Structure into Chapters and Scenes:

Fantastic! You've just divided your story into nine fundamental segments, and now you're one step closer to writing it.

The next step is to take the CHRYSALIS plot you've created to a more detailed level by breaking it down into chapters and then into scenes.

As you can see, what began with three simple questions (WHO, WHERE, WHAT?) is starting to branch out, and soon you'll have a solid foundation to begin building your story.

But before we start discussing how to subdivide your text, let's figure out the approximate length of a novel, a chapter, and a scene.

How Many Pages Do I Have to Write?

This is a question I often hear from people who want to write a book but haven't managed to finish any yet.

First of all, *you don't "have" to write anything*: no one will force you, the Writing Police don't exist, and your fourth-grade English teacher won't come chasing you with a red pen. Your story is yours, and it should be long enough to tell it in its entirety without leaving anything out or beating around the bush excessively. Neither more nor less.

That said, sometimes *size matters*, especially if you're looking to publish with a traditional publisher or meet readers' expectations.

Let's Talk Numbers

Fun fact: Readers often talk about *pages*, but writers prefer to count *words*.

Why? Because the number of words that fit on a page depends on the paper size, line spacing, and font size. However, the number of words is objective: a thousand words are a thousand words, regardless of whether they're written by hand or typed in the smallest font you can print.

That said, we can consider that a page contains between 250 and 350 words.

Novels, short stories, and other types of literary works can vary significantly in length and structure, but ***in general, a novel typically has between 50,000 and 100,000 words***, while a short story can range from 1,000 to 20,000 words.

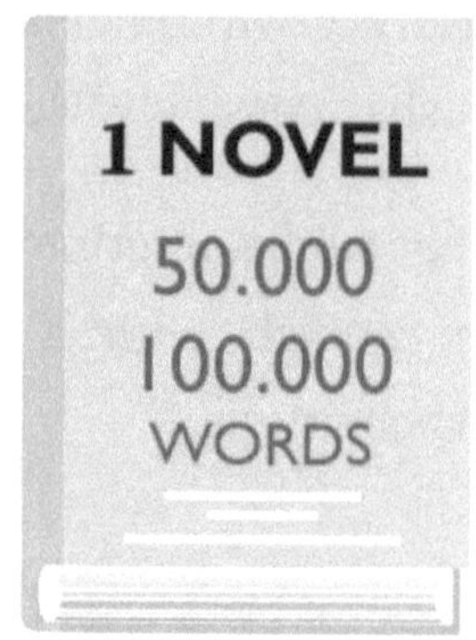

You can use the following list as a guideline:

- Flash Fiction: Up to 1,000 words.
- Short Story: 1,000 to 7,500 words.
- Novella: 7,500 to 45,000 words.
- Novel: 45,000 words and above (some consider the minimum to be 50,000).

We can also take a look at the length of novels by genre:

- Romance Novel: typically ranges from 50,000 to 100,000 words. Historical romance novels are often longer.
- Mystery or Thriller Novel: can vary from 60,000 to 100,000 words, or even more in some cases.
- Science Fiction or Fantasy Novel: generally longer, typically in the range of 90,000 to 150,000 words or more, especially in fantasy novels with highly complex magical worlds.
- Contemporary Fiction: between 50,000 and 100,000 words, but this can vary as there are many sub-genres

and variations.

- <u>Epic Fantasy Novel</u>: usually the longest, often exceeding 100,000 words, and sometimes reaching 200,000 words or more.
- <u>Young Adult Novel</u>: it can vary depending on the target age group, but it's generally shorter, around 20,000 to 40,000 words.
- <u>Children's Books</u>: board books for babies can have 300 words or fewer. Picture books have about 1,000 - 1,500 words, while chapter books vary depending on the reader's age, ranging from 10,000 to 40,000 words.

These numbers are just guidelines, but they will help you understand if the length of your story is appropriate for its genre. If it's much longer or much shorter than the others, you may encounter difficulties with the audience accepting it (for example, fantasy readers tend to prefer "thicker" books and might hesitate to buy one that doesn't have a few hundred pages). Therefore, it's helpful to know these numbers in advance if you haven't started writing yet so you can better align with market expectations.

How Many Chapters and How Long?

In a typical novel, chapters often vary in length, but ***on average, they can contain anywhere from 1,000 to 5,000 words, with the most common range falling between 1,500 and 3,000***

words. However, don't fret too much if your chapters are a little shorter or longer. Every writer has their own style, and there's nothing wrong with that.

A novel usually consists of 20 to 40 chapters, but just like it happens with chapter length, the final count depends heavily on your narrative style. **The key is to keep the reader's interest in each one and ensure that each chapter contributes to the story** with a beginning and a conclusion.

The primary function of chapters is to advance the plot. Every time you begin a new chapter, it should reveal new events, introduce obstacles or challenges, or unveil information that the reader didn't previously know.

How to Divide the Story into Chapters

Short stories typically don't have chapters, but novels, in general, do. However, as always, there are exceptions. I recall my surprise when reading Stephen King's *Carrie* and discovering that it wasn't divided into chapters. I must say, as a reader, it can be exhausting to read such a long text without subdivisions. It feels like diving into a pool without being able to come up for air. Generally, readers need the mental pause that chapters provide, sometimes simply because they allow for a convenient stopping point to go to sleep without leaving a dialogue or scene hanging, and at other times, because they make the story easier to understand.

Many novice authors wonder where one chapter should end and the next should begin. This decision is up to you, although you can use the following tip as a general rule of thumb:

Every new chapter should always move the story forward.

In other words, ***you should plan your novel so that each chapter contains a key event that provides new information about the story.***

If you've used the CHRYSALIS Plot, I suggest that you now subdivide each of the nine segments into two or more chapters. This way, you'll immediately have eighteen chapters, and you'll know right away what they're supposed to contain.

The final number of chapters will likely vary, and most of the time, you'll need to add more chapters in the central segments (Y, S, A, L) because this is where most of the trials and adventures occur.

The Importance of the First Chapter

The first segment of the plot is called "Commencement and Introduction," but please don't interpret the word *introduction* as a boring introductory text where the protagonist only talks about the weather and engages in routine and boring activities that have nothing to do with the main plot.

These first pages are crucial in determining whether a

reader will choose your book or opt for another. Remember that there are many books on the market today, and potential customers will spend only a few seconds deciding whether yours interests them.

Use the opening pages, and especially the first chapter, to clearly establish the genre of the novel and suggest the central conflict or theme. Keep in mind that many readers skim the first pages to decide whether to buy the book, and many publishers will request only the first two chapters before expressing interest in the entire manuscript.

Where Does a Chapter End and the Next Begin?

Let's look at some tips that will help you divide your story into chapters more easily. I recommend starting a new chapter every time you want to achieve one of the following objectives:

- **Advance the main plot**; this includes introducing new characters, introducing conflicts or complicating existing ones, creating unexpected twists or moments of revelation, etc.
- **Develop characters and reflect on deep or philosophical themes:** chapters allow you to explore the psychology, motivations, and relationships of the characters. Still, I recommend including some action in these types of chapters to keep the reader engaged.
- **Changes of setting:** it's a good idea to start a new

chapter, or at least a new scene, each time your character goes to a different place.

- **Temporal transitions**: it's also a good idea to start a new chapter if a certain length of time has passed to make the narration clearer (for example, "2 years later" or "the next day").
- **Perspective shifts**: in novels with multiple narrators, we start a new chapter when the perspective changes (very typical in romance novels told from his and her points of view).
- **Development of subplots**: you can also start a new chapter if you're going to address a subplot, the story of a secondary character, a romantic subplot in an adventure novel, etc.
- **Suspense**: chapters are a fantastic tool for creating suspense, especially if you conclude them at moments of uncertainty. This is a very easy trick to encourage a reader to keep reading.

How to Divide Chapters into Scenes:

A scene is a snippet of the story that takes place in a specific time and place. It focuses on a critical event or interaction that advances the plot or character development.

Here are some examples of scenes:

- *Malia enters a café where a stranger named Johannes is sitting alone at a table. They exchange glances and start talking. At the end of their conversation, we discover they have something incredibly rare in common: they like each other and would like to meet again.*
- *Anna finds an old diary in her grandmother's attic. As she reads it, she discovers that all her ancestors were witches.*
- *In a dark alley, Agent Jack Hawkins encounters the killer he has been chasing for weeks. After a shootout, the criminal escapes.*

As you can see, a scene involves a narrative fragment in which:

- A single event or action is presented.
- The location remains constant throughout the scene.
- The time in which the event occurs is continuous throughout the scene.

<u>A chapter may contain only one long scene or may also be composed of several shorter scenes.</u>

Let's now take one of the previous examples. We're going to create the beginning of the plot and then divide it into chapters and scenes. We'll use Anna's story: she has just discovered that she comes from a lineage of witches.

Following the CHRYSALIS plot, we can start our novel like this:

Segment C (Commencement and Introduction): This first segment will encompass a couple of chapters where we'll see Anna going about her daily life:

- Chapter 1: High School: Seventeen-year-old orphan Anna is at high school, feeling marginalized and different. No one wants to sit with her during recess; the other girls tease her because she has acne and is too tall and thin, etc.

- Chapter 2: Encounter with Rebecca: Upon returning from school, Anna sits down to chat with Rebecca, a homeless woman who everyone else mocks as well, and she gives Rebecca her jacket to keep her warm that night, even though she herself has no other. This helps us understand that, despite being an ordinary young woman, Anna has a good heart and carries the seed to become a hero (she's not a worm; she's a caterpillar!).

Segment H (Herald of Change): This is the point in the story where something happens that will disrupt Anna's routine. Let's see:

- Chapter 3: The Diary: Anna finds a diary in the attic and discovers that her mother and grandmother were witches.

- Chapter 4: The Phone Call: Anna calls her great-aunt, her only living relative, and tells her what she has found. Her great-aunt confesses that she already knew and invites

Anna to her home in Alaska to explain everything she knows. We end the chapter with Anna wondering where she will get the money for such a long trip.

Voilà!

Simple, isn't it? Now, all you need to do is repeat the same exercise with each segment of the CHRYSALIS plot, and you'll soon have all the chapters and scenes of your next novel planned and ready to be written.

SEGMENTS   CHAPTERS   TEMPORARY TITLE

C
- 1.
- 2
- 3

H
- 4
- 5
- 6

R
- 7
- 8
- 9

Y
- 10
- 11
- 12

S
- 13
- 14
- 15

A
- 16
- 17
- 18

L
- 19
- 20
- 21

I
- 22.
- 23.
- 24

S
- 25.
- 26.
- 27.

SEGMENTS   CHAPTERS   TEMPORARY TITLE

Today's Task: Step 9

You can continue planning Anna's story, use any of the provided examples, or develop your own novel in this exercise. Starting with the CHRYSALIS plot, jot down the significant events that happen in each of the segments. Then, on a separate sheet, create a list of chapters. Each chapter should include a significant event, as follows:

- C - Commencement and Introduction
  - Anna at high school → Chapter 1
  - Anna meets Rebecca and gives her a jacket → Chapter 2
- H - Herald of Change
  - Anna finds a diary → Chapter 3
  - Anna calls her great-aunt → Chapter 4
- R - Road to Transformation
  - Anna receives a visit from her best friend who moved out of town and tells her about what happened. Her friend encourages her to make the trip → Chapter 5
  - After a premonitory dream, Anna gathers the courage to ask for a loan from the town's usurer and gets a ticket to Alaska → Chapter 6
- Y - Yearning for Adventure

- o Anna arrives in Alaska, but her great-aunt's house doesn't exist! → Chapter 7
- ... etc.
- S - Shift of Perspective
- A - Aggravation of the Conflict
- L - Lowest Point of the Journey
- I - Illuminating Revelation
- S - Soaring in Triumph

IMPORTANT: Remember that this is just a first draft of the plot. The CHRISALYS segments will serve as a guideline to start writing, but you might find the need to combine some chapters or split others into multiple parts after a while. This is normal, and every story is unique and develops in its own organic way. Go with the flow, and don't feel constrained by the plot you've created. Remember, this is just a GPS, and you are free to deviate from the given route wherever you want. Enjoy the journey!

And above all... **CONGRATULATIONS**! You have just plotted your first story using this method, and now you only need to start writing it.

CHAPTER TEN

Underlying themes

"

"Beauty is on the inside."
—Beauty and the Beast

The heart of storytelling

By now, you should have a fairly clear outline of the story you're about to start writing. The plot is progressing coherently, and the main character undergoes significant personal growth throughout their adventure. You know what you're going to talk about and in what tone; you know how the novel begins and, hopefully, how it ends. You've planned a few chapters and know enough about the characters and their world to write several dozen pages about them.

You've done a fantastic job, and the material you've gathered will be enough to write a book that entertains the reader; it may even turn out to be *a very good book*, depending on the originality of your story and the flow of your prose.

If you wish, you can stop here—it's enough. Close this book and start writing your novel.

But if you prefer, you can take a few more minutes to analyze the underlying message you want to convey with your story and thus turn it into an even deeper and more meaningful work of art.

"But Eva, I don't want to brainwash my readers or sound pushy..."

If I had a penny for every time I hear this whenever I talk about underlying themes in novels...

By *underlying messages*, I don't mean you should hide political or religious propaganda in your stories (although some authors do, and I guess that's fine – after all, it's their book and their responsibility). When I talk about the central theme or underlying messages, I mean **harnessing the power of literature to explore profound and universal aspects of the human condition, universal concepts, and questions that transcend cultural and temporal differences and add depth and relevance to any story.** The inclusion of these themes makes readers feel more connected to your characters because they share those same experiences and emotions.

After all, we are writers.

We are artists.

We change the world with our words because they affect the lives of the people who read us, even if only for the three hours we captivate their attention with our pages.

As artists, as writers, we have the power to convey profound messages that go beyond the adventures and misadventures of our imaginary heroes.

These themes can encompass a wide range of emotions and concepts, for example:

- Love and heartbreak,
- Loss, grief, and death,
- Power and how it changes people,
- Justice, injustice, and the relativity of both,
- Our identity and our purpose in life,
- Our interpretation of all of those and more.

By exploring these issues, you can make an apparently mundane story transcend time and space, resonate with a diverse audience, and create an emotional connection with the reader.

Examples of underlying themes

Let's take a look at some examples of underlying themes in famous works:

- **In *1984* by George Orwell**, the author creates a social and political critique using the theme of <u>government oppression and the loss of individual freedom.</u>
- **In *Don Quixote* by Miguel de Cervantes**, the theme of the fine line between <u>fantasy and reality</u> is explored through the protagonist's <u>madness</u> and adventures.
- **In *The Little Prince* by Antoine de Saint-Exupéry**, themes of <u>friendship, innocence, and the search for meaning in life</u> are addressed.
- ***Moby-Dick* by Herman Melville** touches on themes of <u>obsession, revenge, and the conflict of man against nature.</u>

5 Steps to include an underlying message in your story

1. **Identify your key themes**: First, think about the themes you want to explore in your novel. They can be broad ideas like *love, power, justice, betrayal*, etc., but you can also include more specific messages like *"love always triumphs," "success belongs to the persistent,"* or *"true beauty is on the inside"* (which, by the way, is the opening line of this chapter—for a reason!).
2. **Create relevant scenes**: Design scenes that allow you

to address and explore your themes of choice. They can be <u>brief conversations, situations, or actions</u> that reflect key aspects of the theme you want to highlight. It's imperative to <u>give the reader a hint at the beginning of the book </u>so they know what theme you will be addressing and to repeat it at the end of the book when the protagonist has finished learning their life lesson. However, it's also essential to **do it subtly and without lecturing the reader**; otherwise, the reader may feel annoyed. As the saying goes, readers are not fools.

3. **Character development**: As characters evolve, their perspectives on the themes being addressed can also change. This can reflect their growth and transformation throughout the story. For example, imagine a young woman; we'll call her Kirsten. Kirsten thought she'd never achieve academic success due to a serious case of dyslexia. However, by the end of the novel, she works so hard that she ends up winning a Nobel Prize. The message here would be <u>the value of persistence.</u> The underlying theme for Kirsten's story: *"If you work hard enough, you can achieve anything you set your mind to."*

4. **Use symbolism**: You can introduce symbolic elements into your story that represent the themes. They can be <u>objects, places, or actions that have a deeper meaning</u> related to your underlying themes. A good example is Oscar Wilde's *The Picture of Dorian Gray*. In this story, the painting is a symbol of the moral decay that occurs

within Dorian as he seeks to satisfy his unrestrained desires. While the portrait ages and becomes ugly and grotesque, Dorian maintains his youthful and attractive appearance. This symbolism represents *the struggle between superficial beauty and inner depravity,* as well as *the moral consequences of selfish pleasure.*

5. **Effect on the conclusion**: It's vital that your underlying themes have an impact on the story's conclusion and are mentioned (even if only symbolically) in the last segment of the story. The main message may be the lesson the protagonist needs to learn, or the final scene may leave open questions for the reader to reflect on.

These are just some ideas for underlying themes and how to include them in your story. I recommend reviewing the plot you've planned and identifying spots where it would be easier or more natural to include dialogues or actions that allude to the underlying theme. If you can't think of any now, don't worry: some authors prefer to do this once they've finished the first draft.

In any case, it's relatively easy to include an underlying theme in a story if you plan it in advance. By doing so, you will significantly enrich your novel and add new layers of depth and meaning.

UNDERLYING THEMES

LOVE AND HEARTBREAK

LOSS, GRIEF, DEATH

POWER AND HOW IT CHANGES PEOPLE

JUSTICE, INJUSTICE, AND THE RELATIVITY OF BOTH

OUR IDENTITY AND OUR PURPOSE IN LIFE

OTHERS

Today's Task: Step 10

Use the tips in this chapter to add underlying themes and deeper layers of meaning to your story:

1. Identify your key themes
2. Create relevant scenes
3. Character development
4. Use symbolism
5. Add an effect on the conclusion

CONCLUSION

> *"There was a moment when I transitioned from being an amateur writer to a professional. I took on the responsibility of a profession, of what it means to write even when you don't want to, when you're not particularly pleased with what you're writing, and when you're not writing particularly well."*
> — Agatha Christie: An Autobiography

Key Concepts

We've reached the last chapter, and I want to congratulate you for reading this manual from beginning to end. If you've paid attention and completed all the exercises, by now, you should have a clear understanding of the following points:

- **The genre of your novel:** You know what your story is about and are familiar with similar stories that can serve as inspiration. <u>If not, return to Chapter 2.</u>
- **The main conflict**: You identify and understand the main problem your protagonist needs to resolve. <u>If not, go back to Chapter 3.</u>

- **The characters**: You have a clear idea of their appearance and main characteristics, as well as how they will evolve throughout the adventure. If not, revisit Chapter 4 and complete the character profiles.

- **The settings**: You have considered the location of your story and have descriptions or drawings. If not, return to Chapter 5 and complete the location worksheets.

- **The synopsis**: You can clearly answer the question, *"What is your book about?"* If not, go back to Chapters 6 and 7.

- **The plot**: You have a clear idea of the segments that make up your story and what happens in each of them. You planned a significant transformation for the protagonist, and it aligns with the development of the plot. You have a list of chapters and what will happen in each one, and you're ready to start writing them. Is that so? Revisit Chapters 8 and 9 if needed.

- **The story's message:** Your story, in addition to having a smooth and intriguing plot, contains one or more profound messages for those who can read between the lines. If not, return to Chapter 10.

On the next page, you'll see a graphical representation of the steps we've followed. If everything went well, you should now be ready to begin writing your novel!

 # AUTORISSIMO PLOTTING METHOD

Key points to go from a vague idea to a finished and coherent story:

1

WILLPOWER
Do you want to write a novel from start to finish?
YES ✓ NO

2

MAIN **GENRE**
Do you know it and its conventions?
YES NO

3

WHAT HAPPENS:
Have you defined the main **CONFLICT**?
YES NO

4

WHO IS THE PROTAGONIST
Do you know their identity and what motivates them?
Have you planned their **Metamorphosis**?
YES NO

5

WHERE AND WHEN DOES IT HAPPEN?
Have you defined the time and location?
YES NO

6

SYNOPSIS:
Can you summarize **who, where and what**
in one or two sentences?
YES NO

7

HOW DOES IT HAPPEN?
Have you structured the **PLOT** of the story?
Have you used the **CHRYSALIS PLOT**?
YES NO

8

UNDERLYING **THEMES**
Does your story have a deeper message?
YES NO

Make sure you've elaborated on each of these points.
Once done, it's time to start writing!

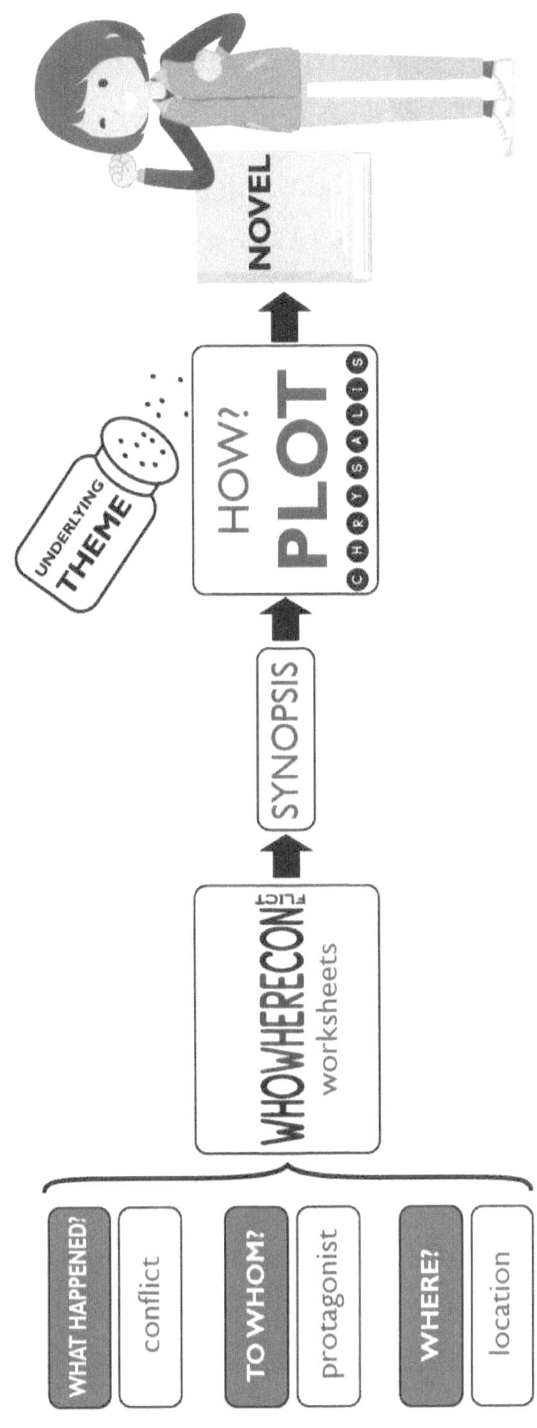
NOVEL
UNDERLYING THEME
HOW?
PLOT
CHRYSALIS
SYNOPSIS
WHOWHERECONFLICT
worksheets
WHAT HAPPENED?
conflict
TO WHOM?
protagonist
WHERE?
location

And... what now?

I can't promise that the advice in this book will magically turn you into Shakespeare, but I hope it streamlines your creative process and helps you plan and write your novels better and faster.

If you'd like to stay in touch, I invite you to send me a message or follow me on social media. I'm always happy to hear from readers and fellow authors, and I respond to all emails as soon as I can. I'd also love for you to join my mailing list, where you'll receive author tips and news from the writing world. The link is: **sendfox.com/lp/3qkywg** (or scan the QR code on the following pages).

If you enjoyed this book, you can continue with the next one in the series. Check out the rest of the titles at www.writersunlock.com.

And now, get to work and start writing your own story. I wish you the best of luck *outside the chrysalis* and don't hesitate to write to me if you complete a book following the advice in this manual. ***I'll be delighted to hear about it!***

Warm regards,

Eva

FIND ME HERE:

- Website:
  - www.evaalton.com
  - www.writersunlock.com
  - www.autorissimo.com
- Instagram:
  - @evaalton
  - @writersunlock
  - @autorissimo
- Facebook:
  - www.facebook.com/writersunlock
- Twitter / X / Threads:
  - @evaalton

Are you looking for more books like this?

Check the other titles in this collection:

Autorissimo Writer's Guides:

Authors Supporting Authors, One Page at a Time

- *How to Write a Novel in 10 Easy Steps*
- *Practical Workbook: How to Write a Novel Step-by-Step*
- *100 Ideas for Your Next Novel*

OTHER TITLES BY EVA ALTON

<u>Historical Fantasy:</u>

- Hidden Notes

<u>Urban Fantasy and Paranormal Romance:</u>

- Series: ***The Vampires of Emberbury***
  - Stray Witch (award winning novel 2020)
  - Witch's Mirror
  - Witches' Masquerade
  - Witches' Elements
  - A Winter's Cobalt Kiss
  - The Vampire's Assistant

- Series: ***Witches of Ibiza***
  - Iris: The Witch's Blood Spell
  - Selena: Wolf Moon

BIBLIOGRAPHY

Works mentioned in this manual:

Books:

"Agatha Christie: An Autobiography" by Agatha Christie (1977)

"Fifty Shades of Grey" by E.L. James (2011)

"City of Bones" by Cassandra Clare (2007)

"The Da Vinci Code" by Dan Brown (2003)

"Wuthering Heights" by Emily Brontë (1847)

"From Blood and Ash" by J. L. Armentrout (2021)

"Don Quixote" by Miguel de Cervantes (1605)

"Dracula" by Bram Stoker (1897)

"The Handmaid's Tale" by Margaret Atwood (1985)

"Bridget Jones's Diary" by Helen Fielding (1996)

"The Great Gatsby" by F. Scott Fitzgerald (1925)

"The Hero with a Thousand Faces" by Joseph Campbell (1949)

"The Name of the Wind" by Patrick Rothfuss (2007)

"The Shining" by Stephen King (1977)

"The Lord of the Rings" by J.R.R. Tolkien (1954-1955, various books)

"The Silence of the Lambs" by Thomas Harris (1988)

"Outlander" by Diana Gabaldon (1991)

"Harry Potter" by J.K. Rowling (1997-2007, various books)

"Cinderella" by Charles Perrault (1697)

"The Girl on the Train" by Paula Hawkins (2015)

"The Divine Comedy" by Dante Alighieri (1320)

"The Time Machine" by H.G. Wells (1895)

"The Odyssey" by Homer (8th century BCE)

"The Adventures of Tom Sawyer" by Mark Twain (1876)

"The Grapes of Wrath" by John Steinbeck (1939)

"The Girl with the Dragon Tattoo" by Stieg Larsson (2005)

"The Hunger Games" by Suzanne Collins (2008)

"Moby-Dick" by Herman Melville (1851)

"Little Women" by Louisa May Alcott (1868)

"Violent Delights" by Chloe Gong (2020)

"Save the Cat!" by Blake Snyder (2005)

"The Snowflake Method" by Randy Ingermanson (2007)

"1984" by George Orwell (1949)

"Carrie" by Stephen King (1974)

"The Picture of Dorian Gray" by Oscar Wilde (1890)

Movies:

"The Da Vinci Code" - Directed by Ron Howard (2006)

"The Shining" - Directed by Stanley Kubrick (1980)

"Harry Potter and the Sorcerer's Stone" - Directed by Chris Columbus (2001)

"Indiana Jones and the Dial of Destiny" - Directed by James Mangold (2023)

"Beauty and the Beast" - Directed by Gary Trousdale and Kirk Wise (1991)

"The Hunger Games" - Directed by Gary Ross (2012)

"Matrix" - Directed by the Wachowski Sisters (1999)

"Pretty Woman" - Directed by Garry Marshall (1990)

"Vertigo" - Directed by Alfred Hitchcock (1958)

Extra Chapter

I've got something for you...

I have a present for you:

Get my eBook *"100 Ideas For Your Next Novel"* for free!

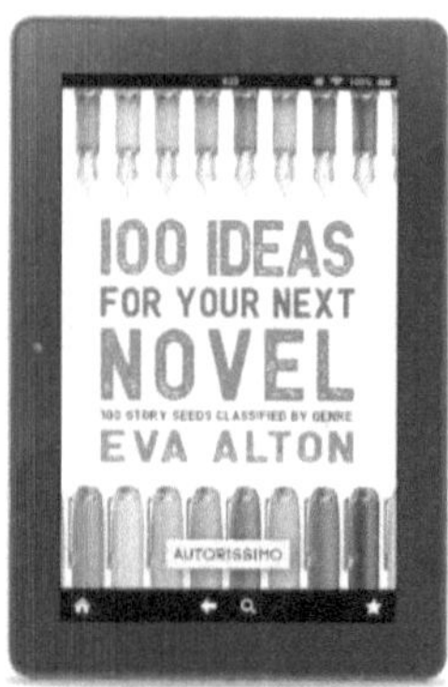

Join my Author's Tips mailing list and receive free materials, writing tricks and much more:

- The free ebook "100 Ideas For Your Next Novel"
- Writing tips
- Information on events and writing retreats
- And much more!

Click on the link or scan the code to get your free ebook:

https://sendfox.com/lp/3qkywg

www.ingramcontent.com/pod-product-compliance
Lightning Source LLC
Chambersburg PA
CBHW060545160726
47991CB00001B/449